ROMPS, TOTS AND BOFFINS

ROBERT HUTTON

ROMPS, TOTS AND BOFFINS

... THE STRANGE LANGUAGE OF NEWS

First published 2013 by
Elliott and Thompson Limited
27 John Street, London WC1N 2BX
www.eandtbooks.com

ISBN: 978-1-90965-343-6

Cover Design: Mark Swan / kid-ethic.com

Typesetting: Louis Mackay / www.louismackaydesign.co.uk

Printed by TJ International Ltd.

CONTENTS

INTRODUCTION

'News is what a chap who doesn't care much about anything wants to read. And it's only news until he's read it. After that it's dead.'

– *Scoop*, Evelyn Waugh

When my friend Tom worked on a weekly Glasgow paper, he had a recurring nightmare that his editor demanded he produce, from nothing and at short notice, the ultimate story to go underneath the ultimate local newspaper headline:

BOSSES
BLAST
CHIEFS!

Technically, this is an English sentence – subject-verb-object – but its meaning is obscure. That's because it's written in the language of newspapers. This is the world of *booze-fuelled rampages* and *crunch talks*; of *troubled stars* and *caged sex beasts*. This is the world of *romps*, *tots* and *boffins*. This is the world of 'journalese'.

WHAT IS THIS BOOK?

In 2003, when I was a sub-editor on the *Daily Mirror*, and the paper was going through a particularly self-indulgent phase,* I suggested that we should start printing footnotes, to give our poor readers half a chance of understanding what we were on about. The idea was not taken up, which was a shame, if not a surprise.

Nine years later, now a political correspondent for Bloomberg, I was sitting in an airport in Jordan, waiting for a 4am flight. This was the government's fault. Downing Street had decided that the prime minister would take a small plane with him on a tour of Arab states, with room for only a couple of journalists. The rest of us had to use scheduled flights, and that meant flying in the middle of the night.

---

* Piers Morgan was editor and, seeing that he had fallen 10 places in the *Guardian*'s Media Power List, commissioned a three-page list of 'The 100 Least Influential People in Britain', where he wrote rude things about people he didn't like. The surprise on days like this was not that circulation fell, but that anyone bought the paper at all.

The travelling press pack had been awake for 24 hours, in which time we'd visited a camp for Syrian refugees, filed our copy, done a mass interview with the prime minister, filed our copy, joined the ambassador for drinks, filed our copy, gone for dinner, answered questions about our copy, gone for more drinks, and found our way to the airport. Queen Alia International Airport doesn't have much to divert the weary traveller, so we sat on our suitcases, told jokes, and waited for our stories to appear online so that we could put them on Twitter. As we finally queued up to board our plane, I sent the following tweet:

> *Travelling Lobby* now compiling list of words only still *in use in newspapers: boffin, tots, pal, frogman, lags...* *#journalese*

At Heathrow I turned on my phone to discover I'd hit a nerve. Fellow hacks were sending in their own additions. 'Vow', 'set to', 'swingeing' and 'funnyman' obviously deserved a place. In its 8am bulletin, the *Today* programme kindly offered 'pledge'. By 10am I had 50 items. At 10pm the political commentator

---

* The collective noun for political correspondents is the Lobby, from our historic right to stand in Members' Lobby outside the chamber of the House of Commons and try to speak to MPs.

John Rentoul mused that he might be able to get a book out of the hashtag, and had to be warned off. The following evening, the list had reached 225, but we still didn't have 'skyrocket'.

For me, maintaining the list became an obsession. I would notice a phrase, make a note of it and tweet it, and then six suggestions would be tweeted back. By the time I'd dealt with them, there would be 12 more. Entire evenings disappeared. I discovered that, to a man who tweets journalese, every news story is a reason to pull out his phone.

My only comfort was the knowledge that others had caught the bug. In the coming weeks, most of the contributions came in by Twitter, but not all. I would return to my desk in Parliament to find anonymous notes stuck to my screen. Political aides would sidle up to me and mutter a phrase before disappearing, or send one-word emails and text messages. At summits, where the British press sit together at long trestle tables, hunched over their laptops, political editors would type in silence, stare at their screens, and then shout: 'Have you got "thinly veiled threat"?'

I applied strict rules for the list, varied only when I felt like it, or changed my mind, or forgot a previous decision: the collection is of words and phrases that either only appear in news reports or that have a special meaning in journalism.

A couple of weeks into the Journalese Project, as it became known, a reporter from one of our leading tabloids took me aside. 'We're worried that if you keep this up, we won't be able to write anything at all,' he said. But I'm not trying to ban words.

Others took the opposite view: more than one person suggested to me that the list could be a useful reference for hacks approaching deadline and short of a word. Help yourselves, but that's not what it's for.

A third use was proposed by the Leader of Her Majesty's Most Loyal Opposition, Ed Miliband. On a tour of Scandinavia that I was covering, his aides explained the Journalese Project to him. He was sceptical at first, but as we gave him examples, he began to join in. When our plane landed with a disturbing thump, he turned to me and said: 'Leader Of The Opposition In Mid-Air Drama.' His team's only comment on a piece I wrote about him was on the headline: 'Surely "woo" is journalese?' an aide commented drily. On the third morning, Miliband came over at breakfast: 'Your journalese game is obsessive. I woke up at 2am thinking "gainsay".'

It hadn't struck me that it could be a game, but

Miliband had a point. The easiest way to play it is to give each player a different newspaper. They go through it, scoring a point for each item on the list that they can find. The player with the *FT* scores double.

But while this book may serve as a campaign for fresher writing, or a handy thesaurus for unfresh writers, or a game for two or more players aged eight and up, I don't see it as any of those.

To me, it's footnotes for newspapers. Finally, readers will be able to understand what reporters are really trying to tell them. Why not ask your newsagent to deliver a copy of the book every day, along with your paper? Then you can cut out the relevant notes, and paste them at the bottom of each page. Or, if you've embraced the modern world, to the screen of your tablet.

WHAT IS JOURNALESE?

'Tecs Quiz Tug-of-Love Gymslip Mum On Murder Bid.' All right, I made that one up. But headlines only a touch less ridiculous appear in British papers every day. They're written in journalese, a language spoken, generally unconsciously, by tens of thousands of journalists, and apparently understood by their millions of readers.

In newspapers, no one ever disagrees with someone else: they 'clash'. If they explain their reasons, they 'launch into a rant'. If they say a rude word, it's an 'astonishing foul-mouthed tirade'.

But this is about more than hyperbole. Keith Waterhouse, whose brilliant *On Newspaper Style* remains an essential guide for writers more than 30 years after he first wrote it, described journalese as writing that evoked the image of a reporter filing copy.* He identified 'tabloidese' as a distinct sub-genre.

---

* Philip Howard's monograph on journalese from 2000, *The Press Gang*, offers a fuller history, suggesting the word was invented shortly before 1882.

These days that distinction is disappearing. The words he picked out as distinctive of *The Sun* and the *Mirror* are found in *The Times* and *The Telegraph* as well.

The language of journalism is driven partly by space. People in other industries probably haven't given much thought to the letter 'm', but we have. It's really wide, at least one and a half times the width of most letters. An 'i', on the other hand, is a little thing of beauty. This matters when you're trying to fit words into a small space, such as a headline. Short words that convey meaning become very valuable. Like 'bid', or 'rise'. So much better than 'attempt' or 'growth'.

That's not the whole story. Some words sound more exciting. 'Slammed' is really vivid. So is 'rant'. Trying to catch people's attention and hold their interest, exciting words are definitely better than boring words.

But exciting words lose their shine with overuse. When we read of 'growing fears' these days, do we have any sense of excitement, or only a weary feeling that everyone's going through the motions, like the cast of a movie franchise that's had one too many sequels?

Then there are the clichés. There's a lot to be said for clichés. They've survived because they work. Journalism isn't meant to be difficult literature, it's meant to communicate information quickly and engagingly, often to people who're not giving you their full attention. Familiar words, phrases and structures can be effective in that. They can also serve a purpose. Writing about British politics for a global audience, I periodically have to find a way to explain briefly some unfamiliar concept or archaic rule. If I find a good phrase that does the job, I squirrel it away for next time.[*]

Clichés can even be enjoyable for the reader, just as a favourite song or a predictable 'twist' in a soap opera can be. A glance through the output of the most popular newspaper columnists suggests many readers must want a level of predictability.

Often, though, clichés are a symptom of lazy journalism, writing that no longer wants to grab the reader by the throat and astonish them, but simply wants to file and move on. We should excuse some of that: most media organisations are cutting staff and expecting fewer people to produce more copy. Sometimes, 'file and move on' is a journalist's job description.

---

[*]   Perhaps this is the moment to talk about 'lawmakers'. No single thing that I write creates as much comment as my references to Members of Parliament as 'lawmakers'. Colleagues on British papers read out my copy in a mock American drawl. And, I concede, it is not a word I would ever use in conversation. But who outside Britain knows what an MP is? If I use MP, should my Irish colleagues use TD? Should stories from Russia refer to 'deputies'? I will buy beer for anyone who can come up with a more acceptable word.

We'll excuse some of it, but not all of it. And we'll start by not excusing 'tragic tot'. If you're going to write about a dead three-year-old, you should do it well, and with thought. 'Tragic tot' was glib and appalling even the first time, many years ago, that someone put it in print. If you find you've typed it, slam your fingers in your desk drawer and, when the pain subsides, start again.

Not all journalese is bad. The inventors of some phrases deserve acknowledgement: 'mad cow disease' and 'test-tube baby' are lovely examples. They take obscure scientific terms, and replace them with vivid expressions that immediately convey meaning. I would give their creators medals if I could.

How is the internet changing this? When copy appears on-screen, the columns are generally wider, meaning that headlines of short words running across four or five lines are no longer necessary. Twitter treats both an 'i' and an 'm' as a single character, and allows 140 of them, space that we would have regarded as impossibly generous even on the *FT*, where I once wrote a 52-character headline.

The ability to publish instantly has also changed the character of journalism. Those of us who work on what used to be called newswires have always been under pressure to beat rivals by seconds. In recent years, we have smiled as newspaper colleagues, who used to see such anxieties as beneath them, have boasted of being the first to tweet some incremental development. These tweets generally begin with a piece of journalese imported from television: 'BREAKING'. It should only be used ironically.

Still, the internet may be putting journalism's business models under threat, but it hasn't stopped the spread of journalese. If anything, it has increased now that readers can effortlessly flick between news platforms. With hordes of young, underpaid and underedited journalists employed to sit on each paper's website, cutting and pasting (sorry, 'following up') rivals' stories, it's no surprise that it's increasingly difficult to tell tabloid language from broadsheet.*

---

* One largely unnoticed effect of the internet has been the redundancy of copy-takers, the typing pools at the end of a phone that used to be in every newspaper office. Today, everyone has an internet-connected laptop, and stories can be written and sent in by email on smartphones. Even 15 years ago, the standard way to file when out of the office was over the phone. When I was doing festival reviews for the *Edinburgh Evening News* in 1996, I don't think they even had an email address. Filing over the phone, often while driving down the motorway or from a payphone in the rain, was good for copy: it added urgency, forced you to get the story straight in your head before you started, and there's nothing like being asked 'is there much more of this?' to tighten your writing.

AMERICA'S JOURNALESE

Three months after I began this project, I discovered that two Americans, Paul Dickson and Robert Skole, had been conducting a similar one, and had just published *Journalese – a dictionary for deciphering the news*. I wondered briefly whether my work had been done for me, but it was quickly clear that America's journalese is a different dialect from Britain's. A comparison of their list and this one could inform a dissertation on the differences between British and US journalism. They have no 'lethal cocktails' or 'snubs', but they do have 'brouhaha' and 'irksome'. They have no 'boffins'. There are only five references to sex, a subject that gets its own section here. They do have 'romp', but to an American, it means something amusing or comic. This perhaps explains why *USA Today* felt safe to headline a soft-news piece: 'Easter Egg Roll: Celebs, tots romp on White House lawn'. In Britain, that would have been a *much* bigger story.

In looking at why journalese is so prevalent, though, it's hard to get away from the idea that newspapers are written that way simply because that's how young journalists think a journalist ought to write. Not only young journalists – I've known senior executives on newspapers who saw it as their job to insert cliché and tired hyperbole into every story.

The problem may get worse, rather than better. As a sub-editor at the *Mirror*, it was my job to cut and rewrite copy so that it fitted into the space allotted, was free from errors, and read well. Newspaper subs are an odd bunch. They work at night, but in an office. They never meet the public, or management, and dress and grow beards appropriately. If you want to picture one, imagine an academic recently released from prison. In the days when their work was treasured by their employers, you would never have picked out the subs as some of the best-paid people in journalism. It always amazed me that some of the *Mirror*'s were allowed past security at Canary Wharf.

There are certainly bad subs out there, but our crew spent far more time taking journalese out of stories than we spent inserting it. When I took the job, in 2000, I was assured it would be a job for life if I wanted it. I left, three years later, to become a sub at the *FT*, and then to go back into reporting, but I told myself that a good sub will never starve. These days that feels less true. Like many poorly understood 'back office' functions, subs' benches are being closed down. I cannot imagine that this will improve either the accuracy or the quality of newspapers.

Journalese: The Case for the Defence

1. It's short, and space is at a premium (which is a terrible word: seven letters, two of them big, wide 'm's; try 'pricey', 'costly' or 'costs'; better yet, recast the sentence: 'It's short, and there's no space'). There just isn't that much room in headlines, especially on tabloids. So we have 'raps' for 'attacks', and 'in' as an all-purpose linking word. Such as 'CRITICS IN SICK RAPS', which fits over two lines across two columns of a tabloid, but also requires translation ('People who didn't like something have made some unpleasant attacks on it.')

2. It's lively. Journalism is writing for people who're eating their breakfast, or commuting, or trying to understand what's just happened so they can make a decision. It shouldn't be hard work. It should carry the reader along, and punchy words help.

3. It's familiar. Busy readers know what 'crisis talks' are without having to be told. Journalese helps them get the idea quickly.

Journalese: The Case for the Prosecution

1. It's clichéd. Some of it uses images that have been out of date for decades. Readers pay for our writing. They at least deserve fresh clichés.

2. Lazy writing encourages lazy thought. A colleague once observed to me that there was a temptation for political journalists to cast every story as a question of which minister should have to resign. The world is a subtle and interesting place, but you and your readers will miss that if you write in journalese.

3. It's unnecessary. The better the actual news story, the less journalese there'll be in the reports. Good stories, told right, in plain English, sell themselves. Journalese is like a poker player's 'tell': it's a sign the writer is trying to make a weak tale look better than it is. Try finding better stories instead.

4. It's code. I know what 'Chef lag is on run' means, roughly: someone who has something to do

with cooking has escaped prison. But I've been reading newspapers most of my life. If we want to win new readers, we can't expect them to learn a new language first.

THE
JOURNALESE
LIST

CRISIS TALKS LOOM WHILE BANKS TEETER

GENERAL

acolytes · supporters of someone with whom we disagree.

afoot · what trouble is and plans are.

after · we will now imply a link between two events that may or may not be related. Or try 'ahead of', 'comes as' or 'in the wake of'.

agonising · what waits are, suggesting that whatever 'tenterhooks' may be, they're not very comfortable.

amid · may be appropriate if **after** or 'in the wake of' aren't.

anxiously · how families will endure agonising waits.

arcane rules · ones we can't be bothered to explain.

Arctic conditions · snow.

avenues · 'And the avenues?' 'Exhausted, sir.' 'Which of them?' 'Every avenue, sir.'

balding pate · generally only used in diary columns and Sunday newspaper profiles.

ban · newspapers are champions of free speech, but we accept that it has limits. Those limits are, broadly, the internet, popsongs, films and BBC broadcasts relating to sex or drugs. Reporters should keep in mind when writing stories under the headline 'Ban This Sick Stunt' that in 10 years they will be unable to explain what all the fuss was about.

baron · oil or union. Never press, unless writing about events 60 or more years ago.

battle-scarred · what a **veteran** is. As with veteran, rarely used of someone with actual scars from actual battles.

bean counter · the kind of person who says an organisation can't afford to do something we think it should do. Within a newspaper, the kind of person who says journalists can't go on assignments to interesting and sunny places.

behind closed doors · where top-level crisis talks typically take place.

bid · it's so short: two and a half letter spaces! And it can mean so many things! Which may be why it gets used so much. For instance, 'murder bid', which as the journalist Gordon Darroch observed, evokes someone asking, 'Who will start me at £100 for this fine mid-Regency homicide?'

bigwig · a **chief** we don't like.

black hole · a point in space so dense that it creates a gravitational field so strong not even light can escape. Or, in newspapers, a gap. Especially in finance, where it typically refers to any funding shortfall over £1 million.

blanket · what snow does to the countryside.

boffin · anyone with a job at a university, a science GCSE, or a lab coat.

bolthole · where celebrities and politicians 'hide out' from, well, us.

bombshell · now we bring you news of a surprising thing that's happened.

branded · a more painful kind of **dubbing**.

branded, immediately · what someone's actions were, by us.

breakneck speed · definitely over 40 mph.

brink · a good way to write about something that would be a really terrific story if it did happen is to write that it's on the brink of happening.

buccaneer · the business equivalent of an 'auteur director'. The ideal person to **helm** a company, presumably.

budding · someone under 20 who's good at something.

By Our Foreign Staff · a little newspaper joke. Of course we don't have a foreign staff any more. We can barely cover Kent. We lifted this from the newswires.

calculated snub · the worst kind of **snub**.

chequered past · they've never been convicted of anything, but keep in mind while reading this that they're still pretty dodgy.

chiefs · we don't really understand business, as a look over our books will confirm. This is how we refer to the mysterious figures who apparently are quite important in it. Typically, a couple of dozen business chiefs will have written a letter either urging or warning of something. Or 'road chiefs', who are especially popular in local papers. But not Road Chefs, a class of restaurant in which no journalist would be seen dead.

clamour · we've written two editorials about this. If there's one in today, refer to a 'growing clamour'.

clarion call · someone has said something with which we agree.

coffers · where organisations of which we disapprove keep their money.

confusion surrounds · we can't work out what's going on, but you're welcome to try.

considering · the all-purpose unfalsifiable policy story. No one will ever be able to convincingly deny that they've considered something. If the thing they're considering might actually happen, try 'actively considering', to distinguish it from the sort of passive consideration people give things before rejecting them out of hand.

corruption · the appalling practice of politicians taking decisions that may benefit companies that have given their party money in the past. Completely different from 'freebies', when companies give journalists gifts, meals, or holidays worth hundreds or thousands of pounds simply out of kindness, and with no thought of receiving anything in return.

cosy consensus · an agreement with which we disagree. Not to be confused with a 'sensible compromise'.

crack · what 'special forces' and 'marksmen' are. Also worth mentioning lower down in the piece that these are 'elite troops'.

crimper · hairdresser. As in 'celebrity crimper Nicky Clarke'. Typically concerned with stars' 'tresses'.

crisis talks · what countries hold as their banks **teeter** on the brink of collapse, and what football clubs have with **wantaway hitmen**.

critics say · we think.

crunch talks · we're pretty sure everyone's run out of patience with the **crisis talks**. We certainly have.

dash off · 1. false modesty about own carefully crafted prose; 2. a sneer at a rival's carefully crafted prose. Or try 'churn out'.

deepened · what happened to people's difficulties last night.

densely argued · good grief, what on earth is this guy talking about?

designer clothes · as opposed to a sack with holes torn in it.

devastating · what 'blows' are, and what we hope allegations may turn out to be.

disinterested · ten quid says we actually mean 'un-interested'.

dogged · 1. The kind of defiance shown by sports-men who spent the match being beaten; 2. What scandal has done to a politician, due to our in-sistence on going on about it.

doubts remain · we don't have the first idea what's really going on, and we've found a smart-sound-ing way to say it.

draconian · the government is proposing some-thing with which we disagree.

dragging his feet · what the person **shelving** something (in the **long grass**) is doing.

dubbed · someone's been given a nickname. By us.

electrify · what we hope today's **intervention** will do to the debate, in the sense of making hair stand on end and causing involuntary twitch-ing, but ideally without electrocuting the argu-ment, in the sense of killing it.

eleventh hour · the time at which one should start

expecting **last-ditch** negotiations or **last-gasp** interventions.

embroiled · the means by which people find themselves, unwillingly, dragged into disputes.

emerged · how people left rooms if negotiations were successful. If they 'broke down', then participants typically 'stormed out'.

epicentre · for when 'very centre' just doesn't sound exciting enough. Even though it doesn't mean 'very centre'.*

expected to · the person in question's office briefed us yesterday.

expenses-paid · for some reason, when they hear the word 'expenses', journalists assume fraud must be involved. Psychologists might be able to explain why this should be.

facing charges · they haven't been charged with a crime, they may never be charged with a crime, but they *could* be charged with a crime.

fancy · what lawyers and accountants are. Wearing silk shirts, probably.

fat cats · highly paid people of whom we disapprove. But never used of some of those whose pay is

---

*   The point on the earth's crust above the focus of an earthquake, since you ask.

highest – rock stars, footballers, actors. Picture instead a man with a top hat and a curly moustache.

foretaste · always a chilling one.

foul-mouthed tirade · someone has said a Bad Word. This event is always 'extraordinary' or 'astonishing' to newspapers, whose staff are well known for their delicate sensibilities.

fresh (of **fears**, **doubts**, **hopes** and **tensions**) · old, but reheated with a new quote.

full crisis mode · a story has got so bad that the subject has hired public relations experts or, if they already had them, called them in for a meeting.

funnelling money · giving it to someone of whom we disapprove.

funnyman (female: **funnygirl**) · usually **TV funnyman**, for why else would we write about him? Consider whether he may be 'rubber-faced'. Generally associated with 'vice shame', 'heartbreak split', or 'secret tears'. NB: needn't actually be funny.

funster · we cannot make it any clearer to you that this person is absolutely no fun to be around whatsoever.

fury · most effective when referring to something basically pretty trivial, as in 'BIEBER FURY', used by both the BBC and Sky in a story about a pop concert starting late.

gauntlet · 1. 'thrown down'. A **back-me-or-sack-me** challenge has been issued; 2. 'run'. They had to get past our reporter and photographer to reach their car.

glug · how champagne is consumed by **fat cats**. Also 'guzzle'.

going forward · the reporter, possibly half asleep, has copied out too much of the press release.

green light · what 'road chiefs' have given to plans for a new roundabout.

grizzled · what **veterans** are.

growing (of **fears**, **doubts**, **hopes** and **tensions**) · unchanged.

guru · management writer Peter Drucker summed this one up: 'We are using the word "guru" only because "charlatan" is too long to fit into a headline.'

hailed · '... and last night tourism chiefs "hailed" the knock-on effect.' As in, 'All hail, mighty and worthy knock-on effect, we salute thee.'

heady · what mixes are.

heartfelt · 1. what **pleas** are; 2. regular in *Daily Mail* standfirsts: 'all parents must read this heartfelt and searingly personal account...'

heartlands · a place that used to be famous for doing something, and is now famous for not doing it any more, e.g. 'Tory shire heartlands'; 'Labour inner-city heartlands' and Chicago, which according to *The Guardian* used to be one of the Rolling Stones' heartlands.

heavily armed · what SWAT teams, terrorists and soldiers are, to the constant surprise of reporters, if not readers.

helm (verb) · the manner in which **chiefs** run their businesses.

hero · anyone who has ever worn a uniform.* Except traffic wardens.

high-stakes gamble · a decision about which we have our doubts.

hit back · disagreed with something. See **hit out**.

hit out · said something. Usually a prelude to someone else **hitting back**.

hopeful (noun) · one who is about to be disappointed, as in 'leadership hopeful', 'Oscar hopeful' and 'Wimbledon hopeful'.

horror death smash · a fatal car accident.

the humble X · all non-human species, on first reference.

ill-fated · frankly, it was inevitable that anything which 'started as an innocent day out' would turn out to have 'ended in tragedy'.

---

*   We may need to think about a new word for people who have committed actual acts of heroism.

indictment · usually 'damning', sometimes 'scathing', and occasionally 'searing'.

infrastructure · either creaks or crumbles.

inks deal · how a company or sportsman signs a contract.

it is not suggested · we can't prove any of the things we've spent the last 600 words suggesting, but the lawyer reckons if we put this line in, they won't sue.

jostle · how people get a position.

journalism's Oscars · used of any award a paper has won. Actors rarely describe the Oscars as 'Hollywood's British Press Awards'.

just minutes away · the distance between two places. The minutes in question can be up to 60, and the mode of transport a fast car on an empty road.

languishing · a particularly unpleasant form of queuing.

last ditch · the only ditch worth mentioning in this saga.

last gasp · even more last-minute than the **last ditch**.

last night · use to add urgency to a story written yesterday lunchtime, or, on a Sunday paper, on Wednesday.

let rip · a **rant**, but with the added sense of someone finally expressing thoughts they've been suppressing for weeks, months, or years. Often written with a sense of sympathy from journalists who know just how this feels.

lethal cocktail · there were *two* drugs in their system, you say?

lifeblood · what small firms are to the economy. Due to a modern medical miracle, they're often also its 'backbone'.*

line their pockets · what **fat cats** do with the **bumper pay packets** they **trouser**.

little Jack · this enables readers to distinguish between this six-year-old and other, larger six-year-olds who have jobs and mortgages.

locked-in · what **crunch talks** generally are.

lofty · what ambitions are.

long grass · where plans that have been 'shelved' are kicked, after much 'foot-dragging'.

loom · what disaster does, shortly before it strikes.

loved one · the good news is that if we've referred to you this way, you're unlikely to be in a condition to care about it.

magnate · someone who has made a lot of money doing something. Reporters are urged to take every opportunity to use this for someone who made their fortune selling refrigeration equipment.

∗   Journalists are its spleen, obviously.

Marmite · what the person **one either loved or hated** resembled.

mired in confusion · what the plans are, probably because of that **U-turn** after the 'wheels came off'.

moggy · all cats, on second reference.

much-trumpeted · our rivals got very excited about this. We're about to enjoy making them look foolish.

mull · they're thinking about it. Well, they *might* do it.

muzzle · any attempt, usually by government or the courts, to suppress the free expression of journalists. It's quite wrong for such bodies to stop people writing what they think. That's the news editor's job.

mystery surrounds · in time, it may **deepen**. Right now, we don't have a clue what's going on.

near miss · really, a near hit.

nipper · bit bigger than a tot, not yet a teen.

officialdom · use this wherever hippies say 'The Man'.

on the line · where one puts money and reputation.

one either loved or hated... · the editor and I disagree, and I have been allowed to salvage this much of my dignity.

opine · what the idiots who write for our rivals do.

overshadowed · what the story we wanted to write did to the story that the people we were writing about wanted us to write.[*]

pal · friend 1. where space is short and we fear going over a line; 2. this is a lively, fun publication, and we're going to use the language of young people. From 1950.[†]

pay packet · what people **trouser**, if it's **bumper**. Or, if they're leaving a job, try 'pay-off'.

pen (verb) · how **humble scribes** give their words solid form.

penpusher · usually found in a **back office**. Not to be confused with a **scribe**, or anyone else who **pens** things.

perfect storm · two bad things have happened to someone at the same time.

Pictures! · newspaper billboards often promise pictures. Sometimes, those pictures will even be of the story in question, rather than a plane like

---

[*]   Overheard in the press centre at a summit: 'Have we decided which story is overshadowing which?'

[†]   The day after she died, we were told Margaret Thatcher's stay at the Ritz Hotel, where she spent her final weeks, had been paid for by 'pals'. I somehow doubt that's how she or they would have put it.

the one that crashed, or the restaurant where yesterday's shooting occurred, as it looked when it opened five years ago.

pins · legs. This story will work best if read in the voice of Dick Van Dyke in *Mary Poppins*.

playboy · usually a prince, arms dealer or son.

plea · a request.

plucky · not long for this world.

plunge · what stock markets do. Or, occasionally people, in which case it's a 'death plunge'.

pooch · a dog, of any size and breed, that has lived up to the best traditions of its species by faithfully and humbly leading children out of danger or helping a pensioner cross the road. *Not* a synonym for **devil dog**.

possibly · then again, possibly not.

postcode lottery · used to describe the uneven distribution of resources, a bad thing. The message may have been missed though, as someone set one up a couple of years ago, presumably thinking it sounded quite attractive.

potentially fatal · well, *potentially*. I mean, a peanut is *potentially* fatal, right?

powerhouse · a business that is doing well.

provocative · Twitter is going to go NUTS about this piece. See **controversial** (p. 46).

quintessentially British · use of Barbour jackets, Elgar and understated demonstrations of approval. Don't use of ITV reality shows.

rabid · what other people's lawyers are. Especially libel lawyers.

rambling diatribe · as opposed to a carefully constructed and tightly argued diatribe.

rank · what hypocrisy is always.

rant · someone said something with which we disagree. Doesn't even need to have been done at length any more, as the *Mirror* demonstrated in 2012 when it used the word to describe a 140-character tweet from an MP.

rapped · in March 2013, a number of outlets including the BBC offered the headline: 'Police Chief Rapped Over Hillsborough', conjuring the image of some kind of appalling duet with Jay-Z.

red-faced · what council chiefs usually are after a 'humiliating U-turn' over parking charges.

reeling · how people were left yesterday by a 'shock blow'.

remarkable reversal of fortune · most of the stuff in today's paper is pretty unremarkable. This, on the other hand, is worth reading.

respected · someone just like you, as in 'a respected doctor faces jail after ...'

roasted · told off.

rollocked · does not mean what we think it means. But it's only one letter away from what we think it means, and that's good enough.*

rushed · the only way anyone gets to hospital, typically after ambulances **raced** to the scene.

SAS on standby · the Special Air Service is always on standby. Its members are also, on any given day, Ready For Action and Prepared To Go In. This is what makes them one of the world's elite fighting forces. The characteristic that makes them every defence journalist's favourite fighting force is that they never deny stories about themselves. So for any crisis, anywhere in the world, it is safe to write: 'SAS On Standby To Rescue Western Hostages'.

scoff · 1. how people eat when they're **glugging** champagne; 2. how experts respond to a particularly daft story floated by one of our rivals.

Scots (Scottish papers) · all intros in Scottish papers should contain a reference to Scotland. All of them. If the story is not, for some reason, about Scots, **stick a kilt on it**.

---

* Pedants: it actually means 'behaved in an exuberant and lively fashion'.

Scots (English papers) · the only circumstances in which English readers want to know about things that have happened in Scotland is if they evoke *Whisky Galore* or *Brigadoon*. Stories that if they occurred in Manchester or London would make the splash should be a page lead at most.

scourge · someone who's unpleasant to people in a way of which we approve.

scribe · a good way for writers and reporters to refer to themselves if they want readers to despise them. For extra effect, try 'humble scribe'.

scupper · see **scuttle**.

scuttle · an alternative way to sink plans that haven't been **torpedoed**. For nautical accuracy, we should insist that plans are torpedoed by outsiders and scuttled by people within a project.

seasoned · what **veterans** are if they're not **battle-scarred**.

secret dossier · someone has leaked us an email.

seized on · they referred to something they said supported their case, but we still don't believe them.

sent to the bottom · what happens to ships when submarines find them. But not, interestingly, to plans when they've been **torpedoed**.

set to (not to be confused with **set to**) · sounds like it means 'will', but if it turns out the story is wrong,

COWELL SLAMS BRUCE ON AIR

you can point out it only actually means 'may'. In broadsheets, outside headlines, try 'poised to'.

set to (not to be confused with **set to**) · **fracas**.

shamed · someone who has had sex or taken drugs.

shelved · what happens to projects that are kicked into the **long grass**.

shockwaves · the result of a **bombshell**.

sip · how champagne is consumed by rich, out-of-touch elites, while the poor starve at their door. Or 'quaff'.

slams · disagreed with. As in: 'Cowell Slams Bruce On Air'.

sleepwalking · the manner in which people look like they're going to do something with which we disagree.

slew · collective noun for journalistic stories.

smoke-filled rooms · where **cosy consensuses** are reached. This has survived the smoking ban.

snapper · a photographer. Or try 'lensman'. Probably they'd prefer to be referred to as 'painters with light', but sadly there isn't room.*

snoops · this group, who are protected by the 'snoopers' charters' regularly introduced by all governments, are people legally mandated to

---

* All these may be used in the paper, but obviously nothing will stop the newsdesk referring to them as 'monkeys'.

inquire into your life, usually your wealth, and usually for the purposes of correctly assessing how much tax you owe without disclosing details to the public. They should NEVER be confused with journalists investigating the private lives of celebrities by going through their bins.

snub · somebody didn't get something they wanted. The number of snub-related stories in a newspaper is exponentially related to its distance from the centre of power. Once you get north of Durham, they make up the bulk of political stories.

so-called · called, but read it with a sneer.

sound off · how somebody disagrees with us, if we're obliged to report their views.

spark · the means by which all **fury** is generated. As in this all-purpose headline from the *Inverness Courier*: 'Police Chief Sparks Fury'.

Special Investigation · a normal investigation, but with a picture byline for the reporter.

spectre · a really scary kind of 'threat'.

spiralling · how things go from being under control to being out of control.

standoff · traditionally, one side will back down.

staunch · what one does to a crisis. Or see Religion (p. 98).

stealth tax · a tax we dislike, and which we will

maintain is stealthy, despite it having been on the front of our paper for a month.

strident · a strongly held view with which we disagree.

sun-kissed · anywhere south of Portsmouth.

table · onto which things are put during negotiations. Plural tables have usually just been turned.

tears · what cheers typically turned to after yesterday's drama.

teeter · what things do when they're on brinks.

tensions · the advance guard of **rifts**.

the mercury peaked · in weather stories, where we'll go on to give the top temperature in Fahrenheit, because it's a bigger and therefore more impressive number. When it's cold, we use Celsius, to allow us to go below zero.

tipped · we're about to dress up our hopes as an unnamed person's predictions. As in: 'David Beckham Tipped For *Celebrity Big Brother*'.

tight-lipped · well, we asked, but no one will tell us what's going on.

toff · an over-privileged product of public school and Oxbridge, who got where he is today through family connections. Not to be confused with three-quarters of newspaper staff.

top-level talks · obviously, there are all kinds of

talks going on all the time. But this report won't be on trivial stuff such as discussions between civil servants about printer paper requisitions, oh no. This is the really important stuff.[*]

torpedoed · what happened to plans.

torrid · sounds like 'horrid', looks like 'horrid'. Doesn't mean 'horrid'.[†] See **rollocked** (p. 36).

tot · older than a baby. Not yet a **nipper**.

tough new rules · as opposed to the soft failed rules that were there before.

towering figure · how the deceased will be described in many of the **tributes**, as they 'pour in'.

tragic · helpful clue for readers otherwise uncertain how to feel when reading of a child's death.

tributes · these generally 'pour in' after a death. Never confuse the tributes that 'pour in' with the 'floral tributes' left at the side of the road. If floral tributes pour in, there's a risk of injury. The only thing more dangerous would be a 'flood'.

trouper · anyone reliable.[‡]

trouser (verb) · the means by which people receive

---

[*] Thanks to Google, I've even found reports of 'top-level crisis talks'. They were about the future of Plymouth Argyle.

[†] 'Very hot.'

[‡] Included mainly because of my fond memories of a piece of *Mirror* showbiz copy that described a celebrity 'swearing like a trouper'. Very rarely, presumably, and even then quite daintily.

unexpectedly or undeservedly large sums. See
bumper pay packet (p. 33 and 113).

tug-of-love · helpful in parental child abduction cases
when we're sympathetic to the parent who's done
the abducting because, for instance, they're British.

Twitter storm · more than 15 tweets on any subject.

tycoon · rich person we don't like.

U-turn · ideally 'humiliating'. Once a fine piece of
journalese that neatly described a policy reversal.
Now applies so widely that we can say a politician
performed one simply by explaining a remark
they made 10 minutes earlier.

unprecedented · what interventions are.

unprecedented breach of protocol · something
involving the Royal Family that hasn't been
done for a while, as far as we recall.

vent · what people do to their grievances.

vested · what interests are.

vowed · said.* Or try 'pledged'.

wake-up call · we haven't been able to get anyone
excited about this story for weeks. Maybe this'll
do the trick.

wall-to-wall · what others' coverage was. Ours was
'comprehensive'.

---

* A good way to give copy an epic feel it might otherwise lack.
'District Councillors Vow To Deliver Fortnightly Bin Collec-
tions'. Should they fail, their very lives will be forfeit.

watcher · freelance journalist. As in 'veteran Vatican watcher'.

wheeled out · the manner in which spokesmen whom we don't like appear.

why I, an X, support Y · a popular standfirst for 'surprising', 'frank', and 'personal' opinion pieces. Usually X can be replaced with 'writer paid by the word' and Y with 'something the editor also supports', saving the effort of reading further.

wide-ranging interview · they talked a lot but didn't say much, and now we can't decide what the story is.

wiped off · the tragic fate of millions of pounds every day down at the stock exchange.

a worse time · when today's news couldn't have come.

wrangling · lawyers, who're rarely mistaken for cowboys, have somehow secured this exciting verb to describe their very dull work. Perhaps they took it in lieu of payment after some especially expensive litigation.

writer and broadcaster · unemployed journalist for whom a £75 cheque is sufficient incentive to come in on Saturday night and do a paper review on 24-hour news.

A QUESTION OF ATTRIBUTION

There are few sacred things in British journalism, but one of them is the reporter's duty to his source. Without these precious people, a journalist is nothing, so sources must be taken care of. That means drinks whenever they want them, lunch within reason, and dinner if they behave. But there is also the question of protecting their identity. Someone's livelihood may ride on no one finding out where the information is coming from. Often, it may be the reporter's. Readers, and more importantly bosses, should be allowed to believe that stories are passed on by a senior member of an intelligence agency, whispering secrets in an underground garage, and

HUTTON'S LAW OF SENIORITY

Anyone quoted in support of a story is always made to sound as important as they possibly can be. To establish how important they actually are, picture the most junior person who could still be described in that way.

not a press officer explaining that the next bit didn't come from him. Sometimes, to conceal a source's identity, it may even be necessary to adjust his language. This is why some sources seem to speak in a voice uncannily like the one in the reporter's head.

according to friends/pals/chums/mates/fellow inmates · according to the subject, who hasn't got any friends to say it for him. Or his publicist, the closest thing he now has to a friend.

clearest signal yet · he said the same thing as last week.

coded attack · frankly, this one would have defeated Bletchley Park. Here's what they should have said ... Or try 'thinly veiled'.

controversial · we like to quote him, but everyone else thinks he's bonkers.

did not immediately comment · we called them 15 minutes before we ran the story.

eminent · any historian we're quoting approvingly.

happy to clarify · the lawyer has explained that we have to say this.

heavyweight · anyone who was available to comment at short notice.

influential · any group who can get a letter printed in a national newspaper. See, for example,

'Parliament's influential Refreshment Committee'.

insisted · out of fairness, we're going to tell you what they said, but you should know we don't believe a word of it.

it appears · we can't stand it up.

it has emerged (broadcaster) · 'I am a broadcast journalist, and I've read this in a paper, and I'm damned if I'll admit it.'

it has emerged (newspaper) · we missed it but it wasn't printed in English.

it is understood · the briefing was 'on background', which is officialese for 'you didn't hear it from me, but ...'

it was reported · we missed it and the editor is cross.

it was revealed · we missed it but we're hoping the editor won't notice.

likely to · we couldn't find anyone to say it will, but come on, it's bound to, isn't it?

observers · a mysterious group, who aren't us, obviously, but for whom we can confidently speak.

pundit · he has no qualifications as such, but he sounds pretty plausible to us.

quietly announced · I missed the press release.

respected · this honestly isn't just the only person we could find.

Sky sources · the BBC.

slipped out · any announcements not accompa-
nied by a press release. As in 'The official jaunt to
the luxurious La Pirogue beach resort in Flic en
Flac cost £1,445, figures slipped out on the De-
partment for Education's website reveal.' – *Daily
Mirror*

sources · we think it's true but we can't get anyone to
confirm it and we've got two other stories to write.

sources close to the situation (business pages) ·
banks plying for trade.

the BBC has learned · we've got Sky on.

the comments made clear · sadly they didn't, but
we'll now explain what they mean.

vigorously denied · when we put it to him, he swore
a lot.

warned that this may mean · we think it's true
but we can't get anyone to confirm it and we've
got other stories to write.

Westminster source · the reporter at the desk next
to me.

Westminster sources · the barman has heard it
too.

will anger · we spent all afternoon trying, but we
couldn't find anyone who actually was angry
about this. Still, someone's bound to be, if we
write it hard enough and put a big headline on it.

will be seen as · we're not saying this is how *we* see it, perish the thought. But some people out there will. **Observers**, for instance. It'll be seen this way by observers.

will enrage · like **will anger**, but with the added factor of the story having arrived after 5pm, or two glasses of wine.

will spark outrage · we hope.

ANATOMY OF A SCANDAL

When public figures are under pressure, the question we're always asked is, 'How bad is it?' With this handy guide they and you will be able to work out precisely how long they've got to go.

blunder · what happened.

bungling · the chief quality of the person who let it happen.

furious row · what we wish to put him at the centre of.

outraged · what customers/voters/fans will be, we hope.

disgruntled · what we'd settle for if they can't manage outrage.

growing murmur · what we'll claim to hear if they aren't even disgruntled.

on the back foot · where his organisation is now.

chorus of criticism · that sound you're hearing is the Fleet Street Singers in full voice.

cause further embarrassment · what his latest action will do for his organisation.

under fire · from us.

barrage of criticism · what he's on the receiving end of. From us.

defiant · he has declined our first invitation to resign.

deepened · what his difficulties did last night.

embattled · he has declined our second invitation to resign.

haemorrhaging · what's happening to his support.

fuel the controversy · what we're hoping the latest revelations will do.

hit out · we got him on the phone in an unguarded moment.

spinning out of control · what we hope this situation is by now.

lashed out · we doorstepped him and he really lost it.

beleaguered · the editor wants to know why he hasn't been fired, when we said last week he was about to be.

death spiral · what we hope his career is in.

climbdown · what all the people who've backed him are about to do.

shamed · his new title now he's finally gone. If any kind of inquiry has found against him, he's 'disgraced'.

break his silence · what he'll do in six months to one of our rivals, or, if he's really desperate, us.

BANNED

This book isn't about banning words. But some journalistic constructions need to be banned. No one would miss any of the following if they disappeared for ever.

admit · banned when used of something that isn't in any way shameful, e.g. 'Vince Cable has admitted that he has a "sensible business-like relationship" with Labour.' The cad.

brave · when used to mean 'very ill'.

bunker · there are too many of these in politics.

claimed · when used of something not actually in dispute.

drama · either untrue or redundant. 'Dramatic shortage' is acceptable only in a story about a city-wide actors' strike.

eaterie · what is wrong with you? Why would you even think of using a word like this?

flagship · banned when writing about dull policy U-turn rather than a vessel carrying a naval commander.

miss · for female teacher. As in 'School Miss Jailed For Sex Acts With Five Teenage Boys'. See **sirs**.

sirs · I know, I know. 'Teachers' is eight characters, and 'sirs' is four, one of them very thin. This matters in headlines. But still, my one regret at never having edited a tabloid paper is that I never had the chance to ban 'sirs'.

soi-disant · are you writing in French, for a French paper? No? Then you're without excuse.

spearhead · except when describing battles from the time before gunpowder.

thwart · unless an evil wizard or criminal mastermind is involved.

Tinseltown · you really don't need to give readers this additional clue that they should hate you, not when you've already bylined yourself 'Mr Hollywood'.

veteran · except for former members of armed forces. It simply does not mean someone who's done their job for more than five years.

volte face · broadsheet for **U-turn**.

FOREIGN CORRESPONDENT

A good reporter never directly boasts about the exciting places they've been to, instead dropping them into conversation in passing: 'That's a lovely piece. I think I saw something similar in Lashkar Gah last year.' Of course, those of us whose visits to Tripoli and Baghdad are fleeting and well-protected should never forget the real bravery of men and women who send back news from front lines. Thankfully, there's little danger they'll give us the chance.

badlands · the bits of a foreign country between the cities.

bloodletting · poetic way to introduce a bomb that killed 45 people.

brutal dictator · one that kills his opponents slowly. If he just has them all shot, use 'ruthless dictator'. If our government could easily 'topple him', but can't be bothered, use 'tinpot dictator'.

bustling · the kind of market where reporters meet lively and quotable locals. Also, sadly, the kind that are targets for rebel bombs and shelling by government forces.

fierce · the kind of resistance that troops encounter as they advance.

firefight · any gun battle we actually saw.

fleshpots · where correspondents head once they're finished at the bazaar.

henchmen · a dictator's entourage. The ones who don't do any killing themselves are 'loyal retainers'.

London · all national governments should be referred to by their capital cities.

on a knife edge · safest way to describe the situation if deadlines mean you have to file from the airport, an hour after you arrive.

one local · my taxi driver. Or try 'locals' – one of the other reporter's taxi drivers had heard it, too.

ousted · the likely fate of dictators.

razed to the ground · what happened to the village the day before we arrived. There may be 'smouldering ashes'.

regime · a government of which we disapprove.

restive · a region that the 'repressive regime' is struggling to repress. Typically, protesters there haven't yet put anyone up against a wall and shot them, but some of them are definitely thinking about it.

rich history · what this 'land of contrasts' is endowed with.

sporadic gunfire · I was woken up seven times last night.

staccato shots · these alternate with 'bursts of gunfire' to 'ring out' in the streets.

tensions · always 'heightened'.

troubled · small country currently enjoying a lull between civil wars.

under cover of darkness · at night. The alternative is 'in the cold light of day'.

warplanes · this is what they call fighter jets in the Middle East. Or, more accurately, this is what we call fighter jets when they're in the Middle East.

war-torn · anywhere where foreign correspondents know a decent bar for every night of the week.

TO PUT IT ANOTHER WAY

bon viveur	drunk.
concerns for their health	because of all the drugs they're taking. They may also be described as 'frail' or 'exhausted' on second reference.
confirmed bachelor	he's gay.
didn't suffer fools gladly	nightmare boss.
eccentric	mad.
exotic tastes	we've got the photos in our safe, but they're too horrible to print.
flamboyant	he's gay.
fun-loving	she put herself about a bit.
gregarious	drunk.
he never married	he was gay.
ladies' man	they never managed to get the sexual assault charges to stick.
well-turned-out	he's gay.

POLICE STORY

Like all specialist reporters, crime hacks come to resemble the people they cover (cops, in this case, not criminals. Well, not often). They dress like them, they talk like them, but we can be thankful they don't write like them. Police statements are written in a particularly diabolical form of English that is apparently required to secure convictions. It is the crime reporter's job to turn them into prose that secures readers.

blaze · what firefighters **race** to.

booze-fuelled rampage · what **vile thugs** went on, to the dismay of **revellers**.

bubbly · how friends described the victim. She may also have 'loved life'.

champagne lifestyle · typically, what someone 'plundered bank accounts to fund'.

children · all violence towards animals inevitably happens in front of children.

clan · the collective noun for members of a criminal family whose relationships are so complex even the cops have lost track.

cold-blooded · any planned crime.

crackdown · the only way to fight crime.

devil dog · a **pooch** gone bad.

drug kingpin · anyone sufficiently senior in the drug-dealing hierarchy that they don't actually have to go out on the streets and meet addicts.

dupe · how **fraudsters** take money from grannies to pay for their **champagne lifestyle**. Or try 'hoodwink'.

fiend · typically either a 'drug fiend' or a 'sex fiend'.

fierce · how we distinguish a serious 'gun battle' from the mild ones, where none of the participants can really be bothered.

firebugs · affectionate term for the people who started a 'warehouse blaze' that killed three.

foiled · one possible outcome of a **heist**. Rarely what happens if a **have-a-go hero** is involved.

fracas · people have 'come to blows'. Or try 'altercation'.

fraudster · one who **dupes**.

frenzied · what the attack was.

have-a-go hero · a nice cheery way to describe someone who, if they're lucky, is currently in intensive care with a fractured skull. Or on a manslaughter charge. See **ill-fated** (p. 29).

heartless · used to distinguish the thieves who steal gifts from kids' hospitals at Christmas from ordinary, run-of-the-mill thieves, who only take from those who can afford it, and then use the cash to buy bread for homeless families.

heist · the means by which jewels, gold or sometimes very large sums are stolen.

high-speed · what car chases are. To distinguish them from 25-mph ones.[*]

hurtle · the way in which cars move down streets in **wild** or **high-speed** chases.

in collision with · a way of getting round the tricky question of whose car hit whose.

inferno · any **blaze** on second reference.

innocent bystanders · the people who **look on in horror** when bad things happen. If injured themselves, they become 'innocent victims', to distinguish them from the victims who pretty much had it coming.[†]

Jekyll and Hyde character · no one predicted he'd go on a killing spree. Probably because neighbours described him as a 'loner' who 'kept himself to himself'.

---

[*]   Periodically, someone steals a JCB, or a milk float. Reporters are positively encouraged to describe the ensuing pursuits as 'low-speed chases'.

[†]   Theologically, of course, there are no innocent victims.

INNOCENT
BYSTANDERS
LOOK ON
IN HORROR

lags · affectionate term for **sex beasts**, 'heartless thieves', 'knifemen', 'fraudsters' and 'drug fiends' once they're safely in prison. Or try 'cons'.

looked on in horror · what passers-by did. If there's a school, or shops, or houses, within half a mile, consider the possibility some of the passers-by may have been children. Unless it's after dark, in which case any children out would have been 'young thugs'.

named locally · the cops aren't saying who it was, but fortunately everyone in the pub knew.

our reporter made his excuses and left · at least, we hope he did. Last time he wrote this, there were pictures on the internet afterwards that told a different story.

plundered · what happens to bank accounts.

probe · what police do instead of investigate. Best of all is a 'murder probe', which sounds like something from a Ray Bradbury novel.

prowler · anyone alone on the streets after midnight.

raced · the manner in which ambulance crews got to the scene, unless they 'sped' there. Perhaps they should take their jobs more seriously.

ring out · what gunshots do.

quiz · what police do to suspects. As Michael Deacon of *The Telegraph* observed, 'every time I see the words "Rape Quiz", I think "This time, Channel 4 has gone too far."' Or try 'grill'.

rampage · what hitmen and drunken yobs go on.

ramped up · what happens to security measures following any warning or scare.

reveller · anyone on the streets after 8pm in a group. Sometimes 'boozed-up'.

scale · what intruders do to walls. I once subbed a piece of copy that described how thieves had scaled the wall around a footballer's house, and then later on mentioned that this wall was four foot high. It failed to say whether police were looking for a gang of dwarves.

sex beast · a bad thing to be. Not to be confused with 'he was an animal in bed', which seems to be a good thing. Typically he's either 'struck again' or 'been caged'.

sex pest · a **sex beast** in training.

showed no emotion at the verdict · what the guilty prisoner did. The victims 'maintained a dignified silence'. At preliminary hearings, it's a fair bet that the accused 'spoke only to confirm his name'.

slay · what 'sick killers' do to their victims.

smut · keep reading for a taster.

swoop · how police arrest suspects, ideally at dawn.

tec · headline abbreviation of 'detective', whose virtues in terms of shortness may be outweighed by its disadvantages in terms of incomprehensibility.

trained negotiators · the people the police prefer to use in hostage situations, because it gets messy with amateurs. Presumably they do the same course as 'trained counsellors'. But a different one, we hope, from 'trained marksmen'.

vice den · where **vice girls** and 'drug fiends' ply their trades.

vile thugs · not nice thugs. See also **vile racists** (p. 93).

wild · what car chases may be as well as high-speed. Ideally, the pursuit should have mounted the pavement at least once.

EVERYONE'S A CRITIC

Nancy Banks-Smith, the television critic of *The Guardian*, whose simple, beautiful prose brings tears to the eye, observed: 'Anybody who can write can be a TV critic for a month. After that you need stamina.' If you fancy a go at criticism but can't write, here are some phrases you might want to try out.

acclaimed · quite good. Or try 'iconic' or 'seminal'.

anarchic · unfunny.

enjoyable romp · although I am a highbrow reviewer, I can appreciate the lighter side of life, and don't just enjoy 800-page novels about men dying slowly in Antarctica.

helmed by · the means by which a 'wunderkind director' brought his new **offering** into the world.

high-octane · a film that features at least three explosions and a chase where a car spins round while the driver shoots someone.

kooky · the best way to describe any even slightly intelligent female singer.

lapidary prose · I started skipping pages a quarter of the way in, but I don't think I missed anything.

mixed reviews · friend wrote/produced/starred in it, but to be honest, it stank and we all know it.

muscular riffing · this is how they get the sound of those 'sprawling guitars' to dominate the 'soundscape'.

must-read · a friend wrote it, and it hasn't been 'panned' by everyone else yet.

offering · what the artist has humbly laid before the public.

outing · another way of describing someone's latest **offering**.

page-turner · it's dross, but we've got to admit, it's compelling dross.

plumped for the duck · what one's companion did in a restaurant review.

ratings smash · the editor's kids like it.

return to form · we may not have mentioned at the time that their last album stank, but let's face it, it did.

richly textured · what an **offering** might be.

rip-roaring · there's plenty of sex, and it starts early on.

singer/songwriter · interestingly, never used to describe Bob Dylan.

sophomore · their second **outing**.

soul/funk workout · you'll really hate this.

tome · of course I didn't read it all – it's 700 pages. But I read as much of it as you will.

top director · hasn't won an Oscar yet.

towering · what guitars, and indeed **offerings**, often are.

THE VARIATIONS ENIGMA

Good style precludes the repetition of a word in the same sentence, or ideally in the same paragraph. But sometimes there just isn't an obvious synonym. Luckily, journalists are kings of the 'Elegant Variation'.* As in this gem:

> 'Clarke, known as "two pizzas" because he once scoffed a pair of the tasty Italian meals at one sitting...'

All of the following have been seen in print:

the battered Nordic island

the feathered creatures

the gas-rich emirate

the grey metal

the handheld communications device

the iconic French vacation resort operator

the iconic native marsupial

Michelangelo's frescoed chapel

the oil and gas-rich north African nation

one of the world's best-loved insects

the popular fish-eating mammals

---

* Also known as 'POVs', as in 'popular orange vegetable' (carrots, since you ask).

the popular microblogging social network

the popular southeast Asian condiment

the red leather orb

the scaly specimen

the secretive Stalinist state

the snooty law chief

the South American OPEC nation under the leadership of the late socialist leader Hugo Chavez

the sweetener

the tasty bread-based snacks

the tasty savoury snack

the torpedo-shaped pelagic species

the vast brick structure

the white drink

the windswept South Atlantic archipelago

the yellow metal

the yellowy colour

Iceland; birds; Qatar; silver; mobile phone; Club Med; kangaroo; Sistine Chapel; Algeria; Bees; dolphins; Twitter; soy sauce; cricket ball; a fish; North Korea, Lord Justice Leveson; Venezuela; sugar; Sandwiches; Cornish pasty; 'the humble mackerel'; Battersea power station; milk; the Falklands; gold; yellow.

THE DEVIL READS GRAZIA

There's a lot of crossover between popular fashion journalism and showbiz, but there are some phrases only typed by people faced with the constant pressure of trying to find a new way to say: 'This one might suit you.'

adventurous dresser · she looks terrible but we're trying to get an interview with her.

brilliantly bonkers · she looks mental but she's too sweet/old/infirm/underage to slag off.

channelling · we need a way to intellectualise her look.

curvaceous · one cream cake or bad dress from **unflattering**.

daring sheer top · which, it turns out, goes see-through if 20 cameras flash at once.

dressed age-appropriate · she's too old to be wearing that.

dressed event-appropriate · really predictable.

fabulous · we're trying to shmooze this person.

fashion maven · one who, even among the 'fashion-forward', is considered pretty damn well-dressed.

fashion police · a group of unidentified people who were rude about her look and who are in no way us.

fashionista · we've run out of words to describe her.

fierce shoulders · scary and a bit unpleasant.

flaunted her curves · look how fat she's got.

had the fashion world divided · everyone hates it but no one is willing to stick their neck out and print it.

jean · all clothing is referred to in the singular. So a jean is a casual 'trouser', often 'teamed' with a 'boot'.

must-have · what this 'shoe' is when paired with that 'sheer tight'.

nude lip · the alternative to a 'gloss' or 'crimson' lip.

on trend · a **fashionista** has hit the sweet spot.

rocking a look · we need another way to say 'wearing', because we've already used that 300 times this issue. Or try 'sporting'.

statement clothes · they're disgusting but by an advertiser whom we can't slate.

style icon · no idea what her job is but she takes a good picture.

subverting · often done 'cleverly' or 'brilliantly', the act of wearing completely the wrong clothes to an event.

taking a risk · wearing something that shows off an inappropriate amount of flesh.

unflattering · terrific! She looks chubby in this one.

HOW WE USED TO LIVE

One interesting feature of journalese is the number of expressions that are now at least 50 years out of date. Is anyone under 40 helped by the image of a footballer making a **slide-rule pass**? Will readers still gasp with envy when told that a pop star on tour 'boarded a **jet**'? You might see this as evidence that newspaper language has fallen behind the times, but at peril to my own life and those of the people I love, I can reveal here the far more sinister truth. There exists a secret society of sub-editors, the League of the Twitching Beard, who are sworn to maintain the illusion nothing in Britain has changed since 1958.* By day, they sit quietly at terminals updating the various supplements that are ready to run when members of the Royal Family die. But after the reporters have gone home, they roam the newsroom, combing through copy and inserting words so archaic that the first Google result for them is a definition.

---

* Look out for my thriller, *The Drop Intro Code*, at the top of the *New York Times* bestseller list soon.

august publication · one that's about to announce that it's shutting up shop after 200 years.

bellwether · only seen in politics stories, it refers to an electoral district that's a day trip from London, where we've vox-popped four people in a pub for a feature on the prime minister's **worst week**.

blackboards · try telling children that these things were once a feature of every classroom, and they just laugh unbelievingly.

calumny · typically a 'vile' one, possibly against a young lady's honour. The only possible response is a duel.

carbon copy · imagine, the power to make two or even three copies of every document that comes out of your typewriter! Witchcraft? No – science!

denizens · the writer has an unfinished thesis on James Joyce at home, you know.

doff · the opposite of **don**.

don · how we get dressed, here in the 15th century.

eschew · a kind of nut, I think.

fillip · what one needs at one's 'nadir'.

flat-screen colour TV · or, 'a TV', as they're now known. But to certain newspapers, still an item of such unimaginable futuristic luxury that their presence is worth noting, especially in prisons, where ideally **lags** would be forced to watch *Britain's Got Talent* on black-and-white boxes.

frogman · usually a police frogman, searching a lake for a 'missing beauty'.

furore · put readers on edge for the rest of the day as they wonder how to pronounce a word they've only ever seen written down.

gymslip mum · doubtless led astray by a 'sex fiend'.

hostelry · where one might hope to sip a tankard of ale.

imbroglio · pretty sure this one only makes it into copy for a bet.

imported car · what the rich and famous drive to their jets.

jet · how the impossibly wealthy get around the globe.

moribund · this one is at the point of death.

mortar board · see **blackboards**.

panjandrums · an invented phrase from 1755. Which should be a clue about whether to use it.

scion · now only used of Nat Rothschild.

serried · what **ranks** of things always are.

skulduggery · I might let this one slide, because I like it, and unusually it sounds like its meaning.

slide-rule pass · the way he kicked the ball evoked nothing so much as a device printed with logarithmic scales and widely used for multiplication and division in the days before pocket calculators.

MAJOR ROADWORKS IN BEDFORD CAUSE PARKING WOE

Svengali · reference to an 1894 novel and a 1931 film. Now always preceded by 'pop', and followed by 'Simon Cowell'. It means, to those to whom it means anything, 'someone like Simon Cowell'.

timepiece · there really are no shorter words for those things you use to tell the time.

townsfolk · typically, townsfolk are worried about what the Count is doing to his visitors up in the castle.

turn on a sixpence · was a sixpence much smaller than the other coins they abolished before I was born?

vaunted · whatever it is, if it's done, it's 'much' done.

Walter Mitty · help readers unable to imagine what a 'fantasist' might be with this allusion to a 1942 short story.

woe · 'for never was there a tale of more woe, than this of Juliet and her Romeo,' wrote Shakespeare. Though he probably hadn't heard this one: 'Major Roadworks In Bedford Cause Parking Woe.'

IN THE BEDROOM

The trick with writing about sex for a family newspaper is to report one or two memorable details – 'FIVE TIMES A NIGHT' – without giving so much information you start to sound like the *Penthouse* Readers' Letters section. The safest course is to spend more time describing the location than you do the act. If you can hear the Benny Hill theme tune in your head as you type, you're getting it about right.

beau · a posh girl's posh boyfriend. Or, used ironically, a posh girl's bit of rough.

bed · what **love rats** and **lotharios** do to their conquests.

bonk · on first reference.

clinch · usually 'steamy'. Means anything from a hug to a **bonk**.

come-hither eyes · how 'man-eaters' lure their conquests in.

courtship · this is not dating, this is not going out or seeing each other. These trips to the cinema are something out of Jane Austen.

lothario · a **love rat** that we like.* Like a love rat, always a man. 'Serial Lothario', as seen in the *Daily Mail*, is unnecessary. If a woman, try 'man-eater'.

love child · the inevitable result of all that **bedding** and **romping**.

love rat · one who has 'two-timed' a partner. Almost always a man. If he's a celebrity, his exploits should be recounted with a slight air of admiration, and he should be described near the start as a 'bad boy'. Also used of adulterous politicians and men on welfare who've fathered six children by five women, though without the warmth. If writing about a woman, try 'marriage wrecker'.

lovelorn · someone who has recently been through a **split**.

menage à trois · *The Guardian* is following up yesterday's *Sun* splash about a 'threesome'.

night of shame · usually involves a **vice girl**. Turn to pages 4 and 5 for 1,200 more mildly titillating words.

---

* Fantastic use by the Wisconsin website faced with the story of a teenager caught shoplifting 10 items including 'Trojan vibrating rings, Trojan sensitive condoms, KY warming liquid and two candles'. Their headline: '14-Year-Old Lothario "Had Quite An Evening Planned," Police Muse'.

nookie · on second reference.

orgy · a game for four or more players. A 'three-some' would also qualify if it was filmed.

paramour · posh girl's bit on the side.

privates · if we have to, this is how we refer to his 'crown jewels'.

raunchy · pornography of which we approve.

reunion · how a couple get back together after a split.

romp · preceded by 'sex', or if we're feeling senti-mental, 'love'.*

sex act · how newspapers always refer to oral sex.

sex session · one or more bonks and sex acts. If it took more than an hour, consider 'marathon sex session'.

stepping out · dating for posh kids.

suitor · one who **woos**, typically in a **courtship**.

three-in-a-bed · always a **romp**. The mental image we're trying to create for our reader is himself (and in these stories it's a he) and two supermod-els. On no account should we suggest that maths allows other possible combinations.

---

*   It's not clear what distinguishes a sex romp from normal sex. I think we can agree though that if, as the *Daily Record* once did, you reveal in the fifth paragraph that 'it only lasted a couple of minutes' and 'was described as "a kiss and a cuddle"', you should probably take 'romp' out of the headline.

tryst · on third reference.
vice girl · a prostitute, but, you know, a sexy one.
wed · the result of all that **wooing**.
woo · what **suitors** do.

JOURNALESE FEAR SCALE

Just as sailors use the standard Beaufort scale for wind, newspapers use the Journalese Scale for Fear, to ensure that reporting of anxiety is done consistently across mediums.

Force 0: calm · fear has abated, but will be back later, e.g. 'North Korean Border Calm'.

Force 1: doubts · fear has been spotted on the horizon but has yet to arrive.

Force 2: concern · fears are beginning to take shape but they're still a long way off.

Force 3: fright · something briefly alarming happened but it was all right and no one was even scratched.

Force 4: scare · a fright that lasted more than an hour.

Force 5: alarm · scare that was ongoing as we went to press.

Force 6: fears · we can't find anyone who'll put their name to it, or say exactly what the fears are, but we've been writing this story for three hours now, and we think you damn well should be scared. Typically, fears **grow**.

Force 7: fear · someone has gone on the record, enabling us to nail down what the fear is.

Force 8: panic · the response to our earlier story about fears has been better than we could have dreamed.

Force 9: horror · there was at least one fatality, and the emergency services still haven't found all the bits.

Force 10: terror · a gun was involved. If a local paper, it was a replica.*

---

* Unless the local paper is from south London or certain parts of Manchester.

24-HOUR PARTY PEOPLE

One of the great skills in journalism is to see the surprise in something that to others is perfectly routine. Many stories come from events that seem unremarkable to the participants. In some branches of reporting, this skill has to be very highly developed. Royal correspondents have in recent years managed to produce sustained shock that a couple who had been together for eight years were getting married, that they became pregnant a year later, and that a soldier in a war had shot at the enemy.

Political journalists don't have to scale these heights, but they do have to affect wonder that for instance, the clever, opinionated people who make it to the top of political parties are ambitious, or disagree about policy. A ritual dance develops, where politicians in interviews attempt not to say anything interesting about their ambitions or views, and reporters note the slightest misstep. In the British government, the stakes are raised by the convention of collective responsibility, which requires all ministers to agree with all the policies of their colleagues. This rule developed in the 18th century as a way of stopping the king from playing ministers off against each other, but is now about presenting a united front to the press. These days, the monarch is just about the only person in the country to whom a prime minister can confide their real thoughts about policy.

aftermath · what there is after a party is **trounced** at the polls. This is typically where the **inquest** takes place.

back foot · what the prime minister is on after his **worst week**.

back office · the bit of an organisation that no one in management, government or journalism understands, and which they therefore agree can be abolished without any damage.[*]

big beast · a backbencher of whom your mum has heard.

bloody nose · what the spokesman who is sent out to face the press in the **aftermath** will say the voters gave his party.

---

[*] Other things that no one in management, government or journalism understands include computer security, the internal combustion engine and the human kidney.

MODIFIERS

Liven up copy by sprinkling a few of these over it to taste:

blistering
brisk
damning
daring
defiant
devastating
disgruntled
furious
hapless
lavish
slumbering
staggering
stinging
stunning
tearful
vile
wacky
withering

chauffeur-driven limo · what government ministers are 'ferried about' in. (Note: the editor has a company car with a driver. This is not the same thing at all.)

collision course · what government departments that differ on any issue are always on.

cosy elite · what they have walking the 'corridors of power' down in Westminster. Quite different from the rich tapestry of humanity you see in the newsroom.

crucial test · what this local election is for the government.

crunch vote · we have no idea which way this one will go.

cut off from reality · what politicians are. The editor's PA heard someone say so while she was dropping off his dry cleaning.

drubbing · how everyone except the recipient will describe the **bloody nose**.

flesh out · to repeat, in a speech, the existing policy, with one new detail.

former strongholds · where the party is about to be **trounced**.

frontline services · the good bit of any organisation, which should be **ringfenced** from **swingeing cuts**, unlike the **back office**.

grandee · they're past it, but we want to quote them anyway.

greybeards · what the Labour Party has instead of **grandees**.

grim night · what a political party had at the polls.

hatched · what happens to plots.

head to the polls · the means by which people choose their governments.

high-stakes diplomatic gamble · typically a sign that **crisis talks** are moving to their final phase, or that deadline is approaching and we don't know what's going on.

intervention · someone famous has written a piece for us on an issue of the day.

inquest · the process by which everyone involved in the **trouncing** will conclude that it shows what they already thought.

kebabbed · after they **locked horns**, the interviewer did better out of the exchange than the politician.*

keynote · what all speeches are.

---

* Introduced to the political lexicon by Neil Kinnock, who told James Naughtie in a 1989 encounter: 'I'm not going to sit here and be bloody kebabbed by you.' The BBC didn't play the quote, but Naughtie instead explained on air that the interview had been suspended because Kinnock objected to the line of questioning, before it was resumed. Thus effectively kebabbing him.

lobbying · the way powerful companies spend money to try to persuade government to change policy. Not to be confused with the vital campaigning work of newspapers.

locked horns · a reporter asked a politician some questions.

long-anticipated · what reshuffles are.

lurch to the left/drift to the right · political scientists have confirmed that parties can only move back towards their base at one of two speeds: a lurch or a drift.

mandarins · senior civil servants blocking something we support.

mired in controversy · the state in which prime ministers find themselves during foreign trips, due to the travelling pack's lack of interest in whatever Important Matter the PM is discussing, relative to the domestic problems the PM doesn't want to discuss.

on manoeuvres · someone is about to **put down a marker**.

politicians queued up to attack · we did a ring-round, and got three.

put down a marker · what a politician does in a **wide-ranging speech**.

ringfence · the only way to keep money safe.

root and branch reform · sacking people from the **back office**. While protecting **frontline services**, obviously.

senior backbenchers · backbenchers who returned our calls. If this simply sounds implausible (because, say, they were only elected last week), try 'rising star'.

shock new poll · finally, the numbers have come back in a way that supports our prejudices.

Sir Humphrey · *Yes, Minister* may have been the finest political sitcom ever made, but it went off the air 25 years ago.* The under-40s demand a new nickname for senior civil servants.

slapdown · a member of the Cabinet that we like has disagreed with a member of the Cabinet that we don't like.

snapshot · what this poll is only.

soundings · what politicians take after they **put down a marker**.

stalking horse · he may think he's a serious challenger for the leadership, but we know better.

strategists · it suits both politicians and correspondents to report that parties have cunning plans to appeal to voters, and that the aides who try to spin them are in fact electoral masterminds.

---

* No, we're not counting the relaunch.

WAYS GOVERNMENT SPOKESPEOPLE REFUSE TO ANSWER THE QUESTION

'I'm not going to get into hypotheticals.' Almost any question about the future can be characterised as a hypothetical one, especially if you keep in mind that there being a future at all depends on the world not ending this afternoon.

'I'm not going to get into processology.' Processology, the study of How What Just Happened Happened, is the study of the past. Which is another country. So perhaps you should take your smart questions to the Foreign Office.

'I'm not going to give a running commentary.' This certainly isn't the time to tell you what's happening in the present.

'I don't accept your characterisation of the situation.' Refusing to accept the premise of the question gets a spokesman out of the rest of the questions about the present. There is the danger that a reporter will ask for the spokesman's characterisation of the situation. To which the answer is...

'I think I answered that earlier.'

stubby pencil · what voters use, after they **head to the polls**, to cause an **upset**. But not to **put down a marker**.

swathes · the collective noun for the seats a party just lost.

swingeing · cuts in something we like. These are not just cuts, they're swingeing cuts.

swivel-eyed · a Conservative MP who doesn't merely wish for a more distant relationship between Britain and Europe, but could probably be persuaded to vote for a bombing raid on Berlin.

throw their hat in the ring · what someone does in a **wide-ranging speech**.

top-of-the-range · anything bought by the taxpayer for the use of a politician.

trounced · what happened to a party at the polls.

tsars · the public sector's answer to a **chief**. Like their Russian namesakes, they're nominally in charge of things they don't really control (drugs, 'anti-social behaviour') and their ultimate fate is likely to be a firing squad and burial in quicklime.

union baron · the elected leader of a trade union. If he's popular with his members, he may also be described as a 'firebrand'.

union paymaster · a **union baron**, as he's referred to in pieces about Labour Party policy decisions.

upset at the polls · we called this one wrong.

vile racist remarks · the sort usually made by local councillors on Facebook, without having thought how they'll look when reported in the paper.

whispering campaign · people have been phoning us to complain about their leader again.*

wide-ranging speech · leadership bid.

worst week · what the prime minister has just had, in the Sunday paper round-ups.

---

* It may say something about the state of British politics in 2013 that 'whispering campaign' was nominated for the journalese list by aides to the leaders of all three main parties.

JOURNALESE ROW SCALE

Every unhappy family may be unhappy in its own way,* but all rows in newspapers, whether between celebrities, politicians or countries, are alike.

shoulder to shoulder · everyone is 'united'. The row is 'brewing'.

tiff · there has been a disagreement that is simultaneously trivial and worth writing up.

tensions · have 'surfaced'. If strong words were involved, they 'broke out into the open'.

spat · a minor row. Does not typically 'expose divisions'.

contretemps · *The Guardian* is reporting a **spat**.

loggerheads · there is a proper disagreement. Readers of the *Financial Times* will be told there is an 'impasse'.

---

* Alluding to great literature in a way that allows you and the reader to pretend you've both read it is a tactic popular with broadsheet columnists. Of course I haven't read Tolstoy. Not even the first line.

clash · the disagreement has been discussed, without resolution.

rift · the result of the clash. At any given time, this may be a **growing rift**.

blasted · what one side has done to the other, by suggesting they may be wrong or mistaken. Or try 'lambasted'.

war of words · both sides are now briefing.

stand-off · both sides are briefing that the other side is about to back down.

bust-up · there has been another attempt to bring peace to the issue. It did not go well.

full and frank exchange of views · how diplomats describe a **bust-up**.

split · what there is now. In ecclesiastical stories, try 'schism'.

row · what 'erupted' instead of peace. Rows can be 'bitter', 'explosive', 'furious', 'stand-up', 'knock-down' or 'drag-out'. In ecclesiastical matters, they are always 'unholy'. Both sides are now 'locked in' the row. The row may now 'escalate', 'deepen', or 'simmer' until 'defused'. With a bit of luck, there'll be a 'bloodbath'.*

---

* No actual blood need be spilt.

PROPERTY LADDER

I was introduced to the journalistic art of property valuation while leaning on a gate, waiting to see if a rugby player whose wife had left him for another rugby player would come out and speak. 'How much do you reckon this place is worth?' the reporter from another Sunday tabloid asked me. 'Got to be a couple of million,' I replied. 'Two-million-pound house,' he said, as he wrote it in his pad.*

architect-designed house · any dwelling where the builders had a plan, and didn't just pile the bricks on top of each other at random.
bachelor pad · a single man has bought a house.
close-knit community · the kind to be avoided at all costs when choosing where to live, as they're always the ones where 'tragedy strikes'.

---

* A rather more thorough colleague recalls attempting to answer the question by going to consult a local expert. 'Sorry to bother you, I'm a journalist,' he said. 'That's all right, I'm an estate agent,' came the reply.

leafy suburb · crime is all the more shocking when it takes place near trees.

love nest · a couple have bought a house.

multimillion · what all developments are. Even a scout hut costs a million these days.

penthouse · any flat above the ground floor.

playground for the rich · usually the Hamptons, but has been used to refer to Davos, Monaco, the Florida Keys, Malibu, Cyprus, New York, Singapore, Aspen, Phuket, Monte Carlo and London. Anywhere you can buy two kinds of champagne.

plush · any hotel where you can't hear the people in the next room.

RELIGION

The Bible tells us that while men look at the outward appearance, God looks at the heart. It turns out that journalists also look at the heart, which enables them to categorise believers. All Catholics are either 'devout' or 'lapsed'. All Protestants are 'staunch'. Muslims may be 'devout' or occasionally 'fanatical', but are never lapsed. Jews are only ever 'observant', though how they use their powers of watchfulness is never explained. Atheists are 'avowed' or sometimes 'fervent'. If they're also Secularists, they may be 'militant'. Female vicars under 40 are 'glamorous', certainly relative to other vicars. The success of any Scottish Protestant can be explained by their 'work ethic', especially if they're a 'son of the manse'.

LIFESTYLES OF THE RICH AND FAMOUS

Writers about celebrity face a particular problem. There's a huge demand for their output, but the serious A-list celebs devote serious time and money to keeping their lives private. Royal correspondents have it worst, but general showbiz correspondents are expected to fill two pages a day. Unlike, say, political reports, much of showbiz output is picture-driven. A photo of Tom Cruise, out shopping and with an irritable expression on his face (as though perhaps he thinks he sees a photographer in the distance) will arrive with little or no explanation. The reporter will then have to write a 100-word caption, without libelling anyone or offering too many hostages to fortune in their speculation about why Cruise might be looking so grumpy. The first five words they type will be '**Top Gun star Tom Cruise**'. Only 95 to go.

all grown up · this caption, about how a 13-year-old actress is wearing a nice dress, was written by Weird Keith, the member of staff we suspect of keeping his mother's corpse in his basement.

ample assets · not sure why we've printed this picture? Perhaps you should look at it again.

clown prince · someone who, while not a professional **funnyman**, definitely just did something funny.

crooner · preferably 'aging crooner'. Val Doonican yes, Bob Dylan no.

defied the cold · she didn't wear a coat.

diva · any female singer, but especially one who wants flowers in her dressing room. Or try: 'warbler' (especially if from Wales); 'popstrel'; 'chanteuse'; 'songstress'.

downward spiral · what **troubled** stars go into.

drugs hell · where their **downward spiral** leads.

exclusive · restaurant where you have to book at least a week in advance.

figure-flaunting outfit · look! You can see almost everything!

flame-haired · not a 'blonde' or a 'brunette'.

flunkey · technical term for a royal aide.

fragile · thin, pale or recently dumped.

glitzy · what awards nights are, unless they're 'glittering'.

haggard · how **troubled** stars appear.

hellraiser · male star who 20 years ago could make women faint by taking his shirt off, but who now is just a tubby drunk.

Hollywood whispers · one drunk person told us but we need to get it past the editor.

little left to the imagination · you actually can see everything in this one.

meltdown · an upset star started shouting at people.

moppet · a pre-teen star. See **all grown up** (p. 100).

plunging top · wahey, boobies!

poured her curves · how women get into 'figure-hugging' dresses.

revealing neckline · not quite a **plunging top**, but there's a strong hint of **ample assets**.

rocker · man from a guitar band you remember from school. Or 'aging rocker', a man from a guitar band your Dad remembers from school. Keith Richards yes, Bob Dylan no.*

---

* On the rare occasions Dylan features on the showbiz pages, he will be referred to as some combination of poet, singer, composer and genius. Sub-editors feel a lot of affinity towards a man who does beautiful things with words while dressing like a tramp.

scantily clad · honestly, why are you even reading this caption? NEARLY NAKED LADIES in the picture!

scooped · how someone collected an award.

she was very professional · utterly cold bitch.

slinky · is it time to do another piece on whether she has an eating disorder?

star-studded · what all events, ever, in the history of showbiz journalism are. Or try 'Stars Come Out For Donkey Sanctuary Fundraiser'.

stepped out · she's left her house, which means she's pretty much fair game for snappers.

swanky · restaurant with cloth napkins.

the smile that says… · a particular favourite of Royal correspondents, this is a handy way of filling caption space when there's no quote, but the subject is definitely smiling. See, for example, 'Is This The Smile That Says I'm Back With Bieber?'; 'The Smile That Says It's Going To Be A VERY Good Awards Season' and 'The Smile That Says I'm Alive!'

Top Gun Star Tom Cruise · or 'Tom Cruise', as he's known to everyone outside newspapers. On showbiz pages he's still regularly identified by his role in a 1986 film. This is to help readers who can't immediately picture Tom Cruise, but will be helped along by the reminder of,

THE SMILE THAT SAYS 'I'M BACK WITH BIEBER'

'you know, the short one in *Top Gun*'. I've even seen Cruise, one of the world's most famous actors, who is never confused with anyone else, identified helpfully on second reference as 'the *Rock of Ages* star'. This was to help a reader who couldn't picture Tom Cruise, even with the *Top Gun* clue, but was still for some reason reading a piece of gossip about him. Rule of thumb: '*Star Wars* star Mark Hamill' is helpful. '*Star Wars* star Harrison Ford' is redundant.

troubled · what stars are, when a **lethal cocktail** looks like it might be approaching their table.

wrapped up warm · she wore a coat.

THIS SPORTING LIFE

Next to sports journalese, all other journalese looks pale. Other journalists may work a **drugs hell** in here, or a **heartfelt plea** in there, but their copy can still be understood. Only sports reporters have managed to create an entire language that is both clichéd and incomprehensible to the uninitiated.

The most impressive thing about sports journalese is that it's not even the jargon of industry insiders. You could know everything about the theory and practice of football and still not be able to understand a piece of football gossip as reported in a British paper. Wantaway starlets, mazy runs, come-and-get-me pleas – players and managers don't talk this way, only sportswriters. Perhaps this is because the writers are fans, not professionals. Few former star players become reporters, and managers and strikers aren't generally recruited from the press box.

Football journalism, which is what most sports journalism in Britain is, divides into Match Reports and Soap Opera.

Match Reports* are an attempt to impose an epic narrative structure on a sequence of loosely connected events, heavily influenced by chance. The story must tell fans that their lives are invested in a great heroic, moral tale. It should also reassure them that the highly paid athletes on the pitch are actually there for the same reason the fans are: love of the team and the game. Why did they win? They wanted it more. Why did they lose? They're jinxed.

Soap Opera is what fills the sports pages between matches. As with showbiz, the challenge for the writer is to find fresh ways every day of interpreting the words 'we're taking each match as it comes, getting our heads down, and focusing on winning for the fans'. Who can blame people under such pressure for inventing a language?

ace · a player who is good at the sport he plays. Sometimes compounded, to specify which bit of the sport he plays well, as in 'goal ace'.

acres of space · there were no other players near him.

back-me-or-sack-me · what team managers tell team owners.

---

* Deadlines are the biggest influence on many match reports. They need to be mainly written by half-time, which is why they tend to focus more on the goals in the first half.

backlash · having been unexpectedly beaten by an inferior team last week, the sporting professionals are going to try extra hard to win when they next play.

bag a brace · two successful shots, an expression used only on grouse moors and in football writers' copy.

best fans in the world · how Scottish papers are required to describe their readers, who only occasionally stab each other after matches for holding the wrong views on Papal infallibility.

bogey team · a not-very-good team that has a record of beating one particular very good team.

booked a place in the final · the alternative to **crashing out**.

boss · 1. to play much better than the other team. 'Manchester Utd bossed QPR in the first half.'; 2. take over as manager. 'Allison to boss the Palace.'

bouncebackability · a shorter version of 'resilience' for people who can't count letters.*

bow out · to **crash out** with dignity.

brave · the sporting professional, having suffered a setback in the match, continued to do the job

---

* It was originally coined by Crystal Palace manager Iain Dowie, and then promoted relentlessly by the TV show *Soccer AM* in a successful effort to get it into the dictionary. It's now widely used without irony. Still laughing, *Soccer AM*? Fair enough, I expect you are.

ALLISON TO BOSS PALACE

they are paid very large sums to do, rather than, say, sitting down and crying.

briefs · Scottish journalese for tickets.

campaign · any attempt to win any trophy over a series of matches.

come-and-get-me plea · what **wantaway** players issue.

coolly · how penalties are scored in football.

crash out · the technical term for losing a game that results in your leaving a tournament.

dark horse · we will now cover ourselves by pointing out that a team that isn't one of the favourites could also win the championship.

disgruntled star · a **wantaway** player on second reference. Typically, he doesn't wish to desert the club, but knows the fans will understand. They won't, because they're fans. He won't grasp this, because he's a professional athlete.

drubbing · what the losing team got, in the course of the winning team's **romp**.

fritter away · what the sportsmen did with their chances to score. Had your correspondent not been stuck in the press box, he could have done a rather better job.

fully 40 yards · a helpful reminder that this is quite a long distance over which to do this kind of thing.

giant-killers · this lower-placed team has beaten a higher-placed team.

glory · what players 'set their sights on'.

glovesman · goalkeeper or, in cricket, wicketkeeper. Sometimes a 'hapless custodian'.

half a yard · all shots that almost go into the goal miss by 18 inches. This is also the distance by which footballers are always offside, and the amount of space they typically found (unless it was **acres of space**, obviously).

handbags · what get swung when footballers have rows.

hitman · a footballer who scores goals.

jinking run · he ran in a wobbly line, to confound the opposing team.

kid gloves · young goalkeeper. See what we did there?

leave everything on the pitch · the manager has requested that, because this is an important game, the professional full-time sportsmen earn their very high wages by playing as hard as they can, for the whole length of the match. Which by good fortune is what they train to do.

lung-busting run · well, it would certainly give your correspondent a stitch if he tried to sprint that distance.

maestro · a southern European sportsman who's especially good at his sport.

mazy dribble · he changed direction while running, thus avoiding defenders.

notch up · what bowlers do to wickets and batsmen do to centuries in cricket.

numbered · what the manager's days are always.

old guard · collective noun for a team's **old lags**.

old lag · player over 30.

opened his account · a **hitman** has 'slotted one home' for the first time at his new club.

paceman · a fast bowler in cricket. A spin bowler is a 'tweaker'.

penned in · a football team found it difficult to get the ball out of their half.

price tag · what clubs put on **wantaway** players.

rifled home · he kicked the ball very hard 'between the uprights' and into the net. Which bit of the net? The 'back of the net'.

reeling · how the losing team was left after its **drubbing**.

roar · the tone of voice in which football managers express opinions, and the way crowds celebrate goals.

romp · the manner in which one team beat the other team by a wide margin. Players who go on to celebrate their romp with a **romp** are liable to make their way to the front pages, especially if **vice girls** are involved.

rub of the green · sporting luck tends to manifest itself in 'slices'.

silverware · what victorious clubs bring home.

slapped · how **price tags** get onto **wantaway** players.

something in the half-time tea · the likeliest explanation for the team's performance improving.

splurge · how football clubs spend money on **starlets**.

starlet · a slightly creepy way to refer to a young actress, and an absolutely routine way to refer to a young football player.

SW19 · how the Post Office and sports reporters refer to Wimbledon.

swoop · the manoeuvre by which football clubs buy new players.

the dark old days · obligatory in opinion pieces referring to the time when football hooliganism used to get onto the front of the paper.

wantaway · football player who would be open to transfer offers.

wire · what the game went down to.

THE NUMBERS GAME

It's very dangerous to assert a number in copy if you don't have to, especially if it's a number you've worked out yourself. You're bound to have miscounted, or forgotten something, or simply not know how to add up.* Much safer to be vague, while keeping in mind that faced with a choice, Always Use The Largest Number.

a host of · sounds better than 'a few', and won't look stupid if it turns out there are six. 'A whole host' works in the same way, except the threshold for looking stupid is seven.

avalanche · just be sure it's more than 20.

bumper · what **pay packets** are. Or try 'cash bonanza'.

countless · best not to use this if a subsequent paragraph will reveal that whatever it is can be and

---

* The newsroom definition of 'genius' is 'someone who knows how to calculate a percentage'. Keep this in mind when reading newspaper stories derived from statistics.

indeed has been counted. And especially if it turns out the answer is 'four'.

droves · quite a lot. At least four **scores**, but not **countless**.

eye-watering · he makes how much? That's, what, 20 times what I get, and for what, banking? That's basically just adding up.

free fall · what prices went into.

inflation-busting · what pretty much all pay rises were in the happy years running up to the credit crunch.

litany · sounds like it should be quite a lot, but generally means one.

myriad · at least five.

package · half a **raft**.

plummet · see **plunge** (p. 34).

raft · the standard unit of 'measures'. Under the imperial system, a 'cocktail of measures' is an eighth the size of a raft. A 'whole raft of measures' is a raft plus a cocktail.

rising · what crime is always doing. The job of Home Affairs correspondents at crime stats briefings is to find a number that has gone up, or failing that to force a statistician to concede that there is a number that may go up in the future.

salvo · a **myriad**, but all at once.

scores · see **countless** (p. 113).

skyrocket · the way in which numbers increase. In the more sober broadsheets, use 'soar'.

spate · six.

spree (of crimes) · more than 10, except in the UK, of murders, where it's more than one.

string · the standard measurement of lovers. For men, seven. For women, two.

up to · look, there's a whole range of numbers we could report, but we're not going to waste your time. This is the very worst one we could come up with. Or try 'as much as' or 'as little as'.

THINGS NEWSPAPER READERS SHOULD KNOW

1. **The number of pages in the paper doesn't depend on the amount of news.**[*] News is lumpy, rather than arriving at a steady rate. But with rare exceptions, papers don't add pages on hot news days or cut them on quiet ones. So a story that might be close to the front on a slow day won't make it at all on a busy day.

2. **There has to be a splash every day.** The splash is the lead story in the paper. Because it's on the front page, with a big headline, it looks very important. Often it is. Sometimes, it's just the best we had. But it has to feel like it justifies the great big headline over it. One of the most valued skills in newspaper journalism is the ability to get a splash out of unpromising material. It's even better if you can do it without writing 'will spark outrage'.

---

[*]   It depends on the number of adverts that have been sold.

3. **Not much happens at the weekend.** That's why Sunday papers don't have many stories telling you about things that happened on Saturday. Instead, politicians use them to float ideas that can then be denied if they don't go down well, and people with something to sell try to get favourable coverage by leaking some tidbits. And daily paper reporters are always grateful on a Friday to be given a good story to help fill a Monday paper that won't be full of things that happened yesterday.

4. **Nothing at all happens in August.**[*] Parliament's away, the government's away, celebs are away, there's nothing good on TV. August is the News Desert. This is why we have the Silly Season, as stories that wouldn't have a hope in March are asked to carry the weight of the splash. It is also why things seem to start happening abroad in August, as suddenly foreign stories can make their way unimpeded to the front.

5. **Not all polls are equal.** Opinion polls four weeks out from an election asking people how

---

[*] Except the Molotov-Ribbentrop Pact, the declaration of World War I, the invasion of Kuwait, the 1991 Russian Coup, the 2011 London Riots. But you know what I mean.

they're likely to vote are meaningful. Opinion polls asking people how they'd vote if a party had a different leader are much less so: it's like asking people whether they'd enjoy a flavour of ice cream they've never tried. But these are at least opinion polls conducted by proper companies according to proper statistical rules. Marketing companies bombard newsrooms with 'surveys' and 'research' of much more dubious quality in the hope of getting their product mentioned in a story. Least useful of all are newspaper phone-in polls, which tend to reveal that '99 per cent of our readers AGREED with what we told them yesterday'.*

6. **Not all academics are equal.** There isn't really an Istituto Di Articoli Grandi in Milan, where spurious research is produced to order for Sunday broadsheets. But there might as well be.

7. **If the headline ends in a question mark, the answer's probably no.** Alan Beattie of the *FT* has formalised Beattie's Immutable

---

* The exception to that rule is the 1999 *Sun* 'You The Jury' poll run after the paper argued at length that Britain should stay out of the Kosovo War. That one found *Sun* readers supported sending in troops by a margin of nearly two to one.

Law of Headlines: If there's a question mark in the headline the answer is either (tabloid) 'no' or (broadsheet) 'who cares?' John Rentoul's *Questions to Which the Answer is 'No!'* has much, much more on this.

8. **There may be an agenda.** There are the obvious ones about politics, rivals and so on, but every now and then a paper makes an editorial decision totally baffling to those who don't know that the editor has had a vendetta against another editor since they appeared on a panel show together in 1996. And it's not just newspapers that have agendas. Journalists are always happy to quote independent experts and officials, especially when they're attacking politicians, but it's worth remembering that diplomats, doctors, senior soldiers, civil servants and academics are all quite capable of holding views and defending their own interests.

9. **There may be legal reasons.** Why hasn't anyone printed this thing I see on all the blogs? It may well not be true. Or it may be true, but true about someone rich and litigious. Or it may be true, but subject to a court order or rules designed to ensure people get a fair trial.

10. **You can usually ignore lists.** Especially subjective ones, like the 100 Most Influential Collectors Of Journalese.* Unless you like lists, of course.

---

* The only reason ever to read lists like that is to spot times when they've got to the Top 10, and realised they left someone essential out lower down, and will have to stick them in here, at the expense of someone else who was very important, but now won't appear at all.

TERMS OF THE TRADE

These phrases aren't journalese, in the sense that you'd never see them in a newspaper, but it's hard to understand British journalism without knowing the language of our newspapers. A reporter never looks at a potential story without asking, 'How will this fit in the paper?' These are the words they use to answer that question.

byline · the most important words in any story.

byline bandit · the person in the office who kindly offered to take down some words you were phoning over, but totally forgot where they'd come from when it was time to file.

embargo · news-providing organisations often send information or quotes out that aren't to be used before a particular time. The benefit is twofold: it gives journalists time to read long reports properly before writing them up, and gives news-providers some control over where the stories appear – a midnight embargo keeps things off the evening TV bulletins, giving them a better chance in the morning papers. Their success depends on their being kept, which with hot stories and the 24-hour news cycle is a problem. In practice the words 'strictly embargoed until midnight' mean 'expect to see this on Twitter around 10pm'.

exclusive · there is some aspect of our report that you will not read anywhere else. Sometimes, it will be the word 'exclusive'.

headline · the bit in big letters at the top of the story.

leaders · every day, newspapers offer small pieces of wisdom which, if only they were followed, would ensure the whole planet was as harmonious and well-run as a newsroom. Unfortunately, no one reads them.[*]

masthead · the bit with the name of the paper on the front page.

nib · stands for News In Brief, a three-paragraph single-column story of 60 words. Usually the product of a 90-minute drive, three hours standing

---

[*] Philip Howard offers the best example of the view that leader-writers have of their own importance. As the world stood on the brink of war in August 1914, the local paper of a small town in the west of Ireland took a stand: 'We give this solemn warning to Kaiser Wilhelm: *The Skibbereen Eagle* has its eye on you.'

in the rain, 400 words filed over a poor internet connection, and five minutes' aggressive cutting by a sub-editor in a warm office.

scoop of interpretation · an exclusive that involves seeing the same thing as everyone else and then coming to the opposite conclusion.

skyline · the panel across the top of the paper with the masthead, placed there to remind journalists that what really sells the paper is the promise of a free sewing pattern (*Daily Mail*) or dinosaur poster (*The Guardian*).

spike · to kill a story. A word derived from the days when sub-editors would have tall metal spikes on their desks, on which they could impale stories and, after a couple of drinks, bits of themselves.

splash · the lead story on the front of the paper, which grabs the person passing the newsstand and says 'Read Me Now Or Die Ignorant!' Or, sometimes, 'Will this do?'

spoiler · a story run to undermine a rival's big exclusive, generally by pretending to have the same story.

spoof · a not-very-exciting front page put on the first edition of the paper to stop rivals stealing the very good scoop that will be appearing on the front of all the later editions, which have much larger print runs.

standfirst · generally on features, an introductory sentence or two with the name of the interviewer in bold letters, but the name of the interviewee not, to remind you who the important person is in this piece.

subhead · the bit underneath the headline, in smaller but still quite big letters, that explains the pun.

JOURNALISTIC SLANG

If what follows appals you, remember that all trades and professions have their private horrors. A quick way to dispel uncritical admiration for the medical profession is to watch junior doctors sing 'Nelly the Elephant' while performing CPR on a dying patient.

death knock · should a member or members of your family die in a potentially newsworthy way, one or more reporters will be dispatched to counsel you in your grief, and get every picture of the loved one that's in the house.*

doorstep · to actually leave the office and confront someone, generally at their home or office. Most fun if they're caught running off on camera.

flyer · a story that we hope is true, and that certainly seems pretty much likely to be probably true enough to run.

---

* This is how I described my job to my wife the first time we met. It was 15 months before she agreed to go on a date with me.

plunder, pillage, poison the well · the correct technique for a **death knock**. Plunder: take your time and get every detail of the story – you may not be able to get back in if you miss something.* Pillage: the story won't work without a picture, so get every photo of the deceased in the house – don't come back without the album. Poison the well: as you leave, say: 'Thank you so much. You shouldn't have to go through that again. Here's my card. If any reporters from other papers come round, tell them to give me a call and I'll fill them in.'

stick a kilt on it · the means by which a story that would be ideal in our Scottish paper but for its lack of the word 'Scots' in the first paragraph is brought up to scratch. Usually all that's required is the insertion of a quote from a campaign group or politician based north of the border, but no link is too spurious.

stitch-up · he thought he was giving me a story about his important diplomatic work. At some point he may realise I'm writing a story about his tour of Amsterdam brothels.

---

* Useful tip: they'll offer you tea. Accept, then drink it very slowly. No British person can bear to ask someone to leave before they've finished their tea.

too good to check · a tale that we suspect may not be true, but we wish to repeat anyway. A reporter setting off to investigate its veracity will be warned against 'a phone call too far'.

vicar · as in: 'I better go after this one, I'm doing a vicar in Leicester tomorrow.' This may only be used at the *Sunday People*, which has a strong line in clerical naughtiness.

Acknowledgements

This book has benefited from many contributors, and I'm grateful to them all. But I should make clear that responsibility for any errors rests with me alone.

In putting it together I've been especially grateful for their support to my colleagues at Bloomberg News, a more enjoyable place to work than we like to let on. In particular to Andrew Atkinson, Eddie Buckle, Kitty Donaldson, Svenja O'Donnell, Thomas Penny, Gonzalo Vina, Reed Landberg, John Fraher and James Hertling, who claims not to know what any of the words in the title mean.

John Rentoul was a pioneer of books-from-Twitter-lists, and supporter of the journalese project from the start. He introduced me to his editor at Elliott and Thompson, Olivia Bays, who with her team made the production of this book much more straightforward and fun than I had expected.

Although I can't exactly recall the 4am conversation described in the introduction, Christopher Hope definitely came up with 'pal', 'frogman' and 'lags' for the original tweet, and has, sometimes unintentionally, offered a number of contributions since. Also waiting for the flight and throwing around ideas were Emily Ashton, Laura Pitel, Tim Shipman and

Nick Watt. If you have to get stuck in an airport for the night, I recommend their company.

Philip Cowley introduced a level of academic rigour to the book, although there are hints that his media contacts mean he is becoming a secondary journalese speaker.

Patrick Hennessey explained Sport to me, and with Robert Watts offered many other contributions, including reminding me of David Wooding's Elegant Variation on pizza. Barney Thompson supplied most of the Elegant Variations, and indeed suggested the category. More came from Andy Gregory, via Peter Sands. Ben Fenton suggested and supplied a significant portion of the Question of Attribution category.

When I started compiling the list, I was pointed to Alison Gow's 'Journalism Clichés I Most Dislike', now gone from the internet, but it provided several additions including, crucially, 'romp'. Several of the terms in the Politics chapter were listed in an *FT* article by Lord Ashcroft. Fahd Husain's December 2012 piece for *The Nation*, 'Adjectivise This!', was thoughtful about the effects of what foreign correspondents write on the places they cover, and provided several good pieces of journalese.

Then there were the people who sent in suggestions. There will inevitably be someone I've missed off the following list, and if that's you, I apologise. There are others, some of them journalists and others politicians and those around them, who made clear they would prefer their contributions to remain a private matter.

Many of the contributions have come from the men and women of the Parliamentary Press Gallery, whose comradeship is often a delight:

Matthew Barrett, Jason Beattie, Rafael Behr, Jack Blanchard, Sarah Bloch, Robin Brant, Kirsty Buchanan, James Chapman, Matt Chorley, Joe Churcher, Michael Deacon, Graeme Demianyk, Giles Dilnot, Andrew Gimson, David Grossman, Ross Hawkins, Simon Hoggart, Patrick O'Flynn, Juliette Jowitt, Soraya Kishtwari, James Lyons, James Landale, Flora MacQueen, Kevin Maguire, Chris Mason, Rob Merrick, James Millar, Tom Newton Dunn, Jim Pickard, Sophy Ridge, Stefan Rousseau, Michael Savage, Kevin Sinclair, Andrew Sparrow, Rajeev Syal, James Tapsfield, Anne Treneman, Michael White, Jonathan Walker, Kirsty Walker and Patrick Wintour (whose disapproval of this project didn't stop him occasionally submitting his own copy).

Then there were the journalists who piled in:

Kate Allen, Catherine Bennett, Hannah Bewley, Mick Booker, Jenny Booth, Hattie Brett, Anna Blundy,

Daniel Bourke, Tania Branigan, Tony Braisby, Ben Brogan, Andy Bruce, Kay Burley, Peter Campbell, Rory Cellan-Jones, Nick Cohen, Christopher Cook, James Cook, Gaz Corfield, Shane Croucher, Marion Dakers, Gordon Darroch, Lynn Davidson, Clive Davis, Greg Dawson, Chris Deerin, Laura Devlin, Claire Donnelly, Gavin Drake, David Ellis, Chris Giles, Brian Ging, Tom Gordon, Vincent Graff, Andrew Graystone, Michael Greenwood, Tom Harper, Paul Heaney, Catherine Hickley, Les Hinton, John Honeywell, Duncan Hooper, Paul Hutcheon, Ed Johnson, Richard Johnstone, Fachtna Kelly, Tom Kohn, Valentine Low, Douglas Marshall, Iain Martin, John Mckie, Colette McBeth, Tim Montgomerie, Laurie Muchnick, Simon O'Hagan, Patrick Osgood, Jenny Parks, Gill Penlington, James Reed, Duncan Robinson, Harry Rose, Dan Sabbagh, Tim Sharp, Robert Shrimsley, Christopher Spillane, Paul Staines, Terry Stiastny, Nigel Thompson, Matt Walsh, Olly Wehring, Michael White, Tom Wilkinson, Chris Williams, Peter Woodifield, Robert Wright.

Friends, academics, press officers, PR people and those who can only be described as Westminster villagers also helped:

Matthew Bailey, Tim Bale, James Barbour, Simon Bayly, Alex Belardinelli, David Bradley, Adam

Corlett, Emily Craig, John Curtis, Steven Fielding, Daniel Forman, Peter Fortune, Suzanne Franks, Al Fraser, Sam Freedman, Tim Gardner, Julian Glover, Madeleine Hallward, Alison Hardie, Jonathan Hewett, Marcus Honeysett, Dave Howard, Christine Jardine, Mike Jempson, Philip Karsgaard, Sarah Knapton, Michael Lea, Iain Mackenzie, Richard Meiser-Stedman, Gabriel Milland, David Mills, Tim Murray, Katie Myler, Elizabeth Oldfield, Michael Paterson, Geraint Preston, Paul Richards, Abbie Sampson, Hopi Sen, Dylan Sharpe, David Skelton, Jacqui Smith, Ed Staite, Stefan Stern, James Stewart, Ibrahim Taguri, Steve Van Riel, Andy Walton, Giles Wilkes, Stewart Wood, John Woodcock, Simon Wren, Kenny Young.

And I'm finally grateful to the people of Twitter who showed unstinting enthusiasm for the project. In some cases, I don't have a real name, but they're known unto the internet:

@Andrew182651, @bbqbobs, @bilbocroft, @BristleKRS, @citizen_sane, @forwardnotback, @Infamyinforme, @letweetcestmoi, @Nickinthecity, @MsNicolaLucas, @PeterJQJ, @plaintexters, @ralasdair, @realpolitikhome, James Allen, John Avery, Chris Bell, Asa Bennett, Chloe Bidos, Ed Caesar, George Cazenove, Sam Clack, Andrew Denny,

Allan Draycott, Alex Dunlop, Nicky Edwards, Mark Ferguson, Colin Forster, David Hall-Matthews, John Hitchin, Adam Hurrey, David Johnston, Robert Kaye, Maggie Lavan, Omer Lev, David Lucas, Sam MacAuslan, Steven Maloney, Della Mirandola, Sean Mulcahy, Kevin Meagher, Peter Morley, Ian Moss, Thomas Neumark, Gareth Nicholson, Matt Nixon, Brian Nolan, Daniel Olive, James Robinson, Daniela Sacerdoti, Niall Smith, Stephen Smith, Thomas Singlehurst, Ben Stanley, Tom Startup, Jessica Studdert, Adam Tyndall, Luke Tyson, N Von Ho, Peter Walker, Peter Warner, Danny Webster, Oliver Wilkinson, Max Wilkinson.

My wife Sophie played the roles of editor, technical adviser and judger of jokes with unflagging enthusiasm. Her own book has pictures of cowboys in it, and will be of more immediate interest to our sons Fraser and Cameron. But I hope when they're older they'll like mine, too.

My greatest debt is to my mother, Sue Hutton-Squire, whose tales of her days as a secretary in a Sydney newsroom first made me wide-eyed at the idea of a journalist's life. In one of our final conversations in 2012, she reminded me that I'd once been a humorous writer, quoting to me a joke I'd made 18 years earlier. She loved the English language, and I think this is a book she would have enjoyed.

About the author

Robert Hutton has been UK political correspondent for Bloomberg since 2004; previously, he worked at the *Mirror* and *Financial Times*. Arguably his most notable contribution to journalism has been the introduction of the 'news sandwich' to the political lexicon. He lives in south-east London with his wife and two sons.

If you enjoyed this book, you may also like

The Banned List:
A Manifesto Against Jargon and Cliché

By John Rentoul

The Banned List began with five clichés, and has grown steadily ever since. Here, its creator John Rentoul sets out the need for such a list and argues the case for clear writing. He looks at the lure of the cliché and how jargon from different walks of life has made its way into the language everyone uses. Cloudy, meaningless words and tired, hackneyed phrases are not merely annoying, they make it harder for us to communicate.

The solution is simple, however. *The Banned List* shows you the traps to avoid and the rules to bear in mind when writing or speaking clearly and simply. It also contains The List in full. Keep it close to hand at all times and you can't go wrong.